# Two Things

*By* Louise Caudle

PublishAmerica
Baltimore

First printing



Softcover: 978-1-4489-9184-6
PUBLISHED BY PUBLISHAMERICA, LLLP
www.publishamerica.com
Baltimore

Printed in the United States of America

*Dedicated to the memory of Martha and L.L. who set the path*
*And to Martha Ann who kept me on it.*

# Acknowledgments

The principal medical information came from Carolinas Medical Center and Charlotte Institute of Rehabilitation (now Carolinas Rehabilitation). Thanks go out to the doctors, nurses, therapists, and staff members of these facilities. Special thanks go out to Louis, the emergency room Chaplin, Dr. Wattenbarger with the Miller Orthopedic Clinic, and Paul Smith with The Charlotte Institute of Rehabilitation. I wish to thank Mary Brand for her encouragement, prayers, and for directing me to PublishAmerica. I also wish to thank Kristin Trick, my editor and photographer, and Rosalind Eaves, my "second printing" editor Others who have been very helpful include, but are not limited to, Center United Methodist Church, Pastor Queen, the local newspaper, local fire department, my friends, relatives, and colleagues. I wish to thank anyone who said a prayer during any of the circumstances found in this book, but, mostly, I wish to thank the Lord God Almighty for His loving care. To Him goes all the praise and glory.

# Introduction

Her sister was dying. Everyone was sure of it. The doctor said six months to a year was the median time for such tumors and that since Dianne's was the size of a baseball, she would be on the short side. All the radiation treatments would only slow the growth. It had roots, some said tentacles. Laura could imagine the tentacles, an evil thing that would take the life away from her sister. Yes, "tentacles" was a much more descriptive word for the situation. The surgery removed two-thirds of the tumor along with the entire left frontal lobe and bought them some time, but not much. The demon would continue to grow.

The amazing part was the attitude of Dianne. She was so pleased to have her vision back. She said, "I feel a lot stronger not seeing two of everything. I'll be able to do more now; maybe I can fix the sandwiches for lunch. Oh, and did you find the Jimmy Buffett tickets? You need to bring them with you next weekend and leave ours here. Y'all will probably leave from there and we'll meet in Raleigh." The Buffett concert was a big deal. It would entail the usual massive effort and would provide the same release that it always did. Rain or shine, good seats or bad, or lawn under the stars or in the downpour, it did not matter. A good time was to be had by all. Dianne started the whole thing years before, when, under the influence of Kevin, her oldest child, she began taking Laura to the concerts to celebrate her birthday. This year would be really special. Laura had spent hours on the phone, because the Internet site was no good for wheelchair access, and finally secured the magic eight tickets. Laura and Dianne planned for everyday to be a celebration.

Dianne was of the mind, "I've had fifty-six good years. Lots of people live a hundred years and don't have what I have had. I just can't believe I've got this thing in my head. What makes me crazy is that no one will tell me how long I have. Is it a month? A year? Will I make it through the summer? Do you know?"

"No," Laura replied, "No one really knows for sure. Even if they did know, they wouldn't tell you for fear you would get to that day and just quit."

"Oh, yeah, I can see it now. They ought to know me better than that. What do they think, that I'll get to that day and say, 'Okay, its time to quit, clunk'?"

Laura had to laugh. It was fun just resting on the bed beside Dianne and discussing what life was offering now. "You know, Dianne, people are pretty upset about all this. I have been more upset than you could possibly imagine."

"I know". Then Dianne spoke of her husband, Charles, and her two sons, Kevin, aged 25, and Brad, aged 21. "Charles and Kevin and Brad are real upset too. Charles says he doesn't think I'm taking it seriously enough. I think it must be harder on the families than on the sick person."

"Well, we need to make each day count. We need to celebrate every day that we have."

"You're right. We will celebrate."

"We will have a good time at the Buffett concert."

"Yes, and we'll have a good Easter dinner. Did you find the Easter baskets upstairs?"

"Yep. Don't worry about anything. It's all taken care of."

"Good."

That had been the conversation three weeks ago and another weekend in Wilmington was being planned. Laura intended to spend as much time with her sister as possible, even if it was hard to do. She had informed her family to expect to spend a lot of time in Wilmington over the next six months. What's a four-hour drive when time was so precious? And if some other things had to wait, so what? The pain of this situation was close to unbearable. It had really thrown Laura for a loop. Another loop. She was still reeling from the first loop. It was hard to crawl back from the blow. As she questioned and prayed and questioned and prayed the only answer that came back to her was "Write the book." People had been telling Laura for years that she should write a book, a book about handling bad things with a good attitude. Dianne had even asked her on one occasion if she felt that she was being tested for some reason. The book kept popping up. Should it be a whinny, a sexy and steamy, or what kind of book? Now, Laura was convinced that glory should be given to the Lord for her blessings, and the book could do it.

# Who Is Laura, Anyway?

Laura was a baby boomer, born in 1946. Her sister, Dianne, was almost four years old at the time. Her mother had worked as a proofreader for a book company up until Dianne was born. Her father was chief engineer at a local radio station. Her parents had been married for nine years when she was born.

When Laura was two, Dad made them spend the entire summer inside the house because the polio epidemic was so bad. A child in their neighborhood had actually died.

When Laura was six, the family moved to a three-bedroom house on the next street. Mom and Dad had property across town in a really nice section, but Dianne and Laura cried every time they left the neighborhood. There were nine other children their age within walking distance of their house. Nobody really wanted to give that up, so the family moved one block over.

Soon after that, Laura misunderstood some directions, and thinking that she was suppose to wait and walk home from school with her sister, got tired of waiting and started the walk alone. Instead of crossing the busy intersection (the crossing guard was not on duty now) she just turned right and started heading for home. She walked about four miles. Finally, a construction worker asked where she was going since there was nothing left but empty highway. He flagged down a man driving with his family and told him about Laura. The man put her in his car and retraced Laura's steps until she recognized something. Well, when they turned onto Laura's street the whole neighborhood was out looking for her. Mom was hysterical and Dad was home from work. They were very grateful that this family had brought Laura home and not kidnapped her or worse. Laura explained what she had overheard her Mom say on the phone. What she had not heard was that Laura was supposed to wait at the neighbor's house down the street and walk home with Dianne from there.

Laura's childhood was close to perfect. Her parents did not argue. Her Mom made their clothes and taught her girls to sew. They shared chores, had company, and played with friends. Dad built a swing set and a small swimming pool. They visited with family and went to church. They ate supper every night at six, on the breezeway whenever possible. Dad built a brick grill, and they had the neighbors over for barbeque chicken. They went on super vacations to the mountains because a man Dad worked for owned a house there or they went to the beach and shared a house with some cousins. They had great birthday parties. Dianne and Laura could always have a party. Mom and Dad were also involved with school. Mom was forever a grade mother and on the PTA, and Dad installed the intercom system. Laura got to help each morning getting the lunch and milk count from each room using the new system. They did not spend a lot of money, because there was not a lot of money to spend.

They spent time at the river, where Dad had leased some property before he had married and at some point built a one-room cabin. It did not have a bathroom or running water, but it had a nice screened-in porch. There was an outhouse and storage shed. They would swim and fish all day. At night they would grill and if the weather held, they could spend the night. When Laura was nine she caught a three-pound bass while trolling with her Dad in their little fishing boat with a seven and a half horsepower motor. Mom fried the fish in pancake batter. Pancake batter… No one expected anything like that fish!

In 1957, the radio station also became at TV station. Dad was still chief engineer and had made many trips to Washington working with the FCC. It was to be a real plus for their family. Dad started drawing plans and working with architects on the new TV station. The company gave them a color TV and people came to watch all the time. New Year's Day was a big event, as was the Chevy Show, Bonanza and some boring show on Sunday—all brought to you in living color by the NBC peacock. It was very similar to getting the first black and white TV when Laura was four. All the neighborhood kids would look in the living room window to see the Indian test pattern. The big kids would hold the little ones on their shoulders so they could have a better view.

In 1959, they broke ground for the new TV station, and Dad had some people add onto the river cabin. Laura felt that these two events were connected in some way because the windows were exactly alike. Dad was very busy so his girls painted the cabin as best they could. They painted it pink.

The whole family was spending way too much time in a dentist chair. It seems like they had been going to a bad dentist. Everybody had cavities. Dianne had an abscessed tooth; her Dad had four. Does anyone out there know what four abscess teeth and stress from work can do to your body?

Dianne went off to college and Laura missed her something awful. Sometimes she would go to visit. Dianne always had her fixed up with some great guy and threatened his life if he misbehaved.

On March 17, 1962, Saint Patrick's Day, Laura and her Mom went shopping for Easter clothes. They were not much into it and finally returned home to pick out some patterns to make their outfits. Dad was stretched out in the car resting from yard work. He came into the house with them and went back to the bedroom. When Laura went to the bedroom to look for some patterns, her Dad said, "Laura, tell your mother to call the doctor."

Laura told her Mom and Mom flew into action, because Dad had never said anything like that before. He was always in good health. Though he smoked, six months before he had undergone a complete physical and everything was fine. Mom called the doctor and told him how her husband was feeling only to have to call an ambulance. Then she helped her life's love to the bathroom. Laura went outside to wait on the ambulance and explain to neighbors what was happening, so they could help call some relatives.

They waited outside the emergency room. Dr. Harley called them aside to say that C.C., Dad, had suffered a major heart attack. Laura started to cry. Dr. Harley told her to save her tears for when she needed them. Right now, they could go see her Dad for a minute before they took him upstairs. Her father spoke to them, but he was very uncomfortable.

The first person to the hospital was the TV station President. Many others soon followed; more than thirty people. Laura's aunt and cousins were on their way from Atlanta. Dianne was making plans to come home.

In an hour or so they got to go upstairs to see Dad. He was in an oxygen tent. Explaining what would happen if he tried to smoke inside the tent, he proclaimed that his smoking days were over. They were only given a minute and then the nurses led them out of the room.

Everyone felt better with the news of the visit. Glad to greet her with some good news, some neighbors left for the airport to pick up Dianne.

Not thirty minutes later, Dr. Harley came to say that there had been another massive heart attack. Her Dad was dead at fifty years old. Mom was only forty-eight.

Dianne came in from the airport. Someone gave Laura a shot to calm her down. Eventually, they went home. The neighbors had cleaned up the house. Relatives spent the night. There were many, many visitors and hundreds of people at the funeral. Laura stayed out of school for a week. Quiet in the house, she still listened for Dad's car to come in the driveway.

Though it was six months before the stream of visitors ceased, Mom could not bear to go to church. When she tried, she ended up upset, and they would have to leave. Because she could not eat, she quit cooking. Laura thought they would both starve to death so she started fixing the meals. Laura took on as many of her Dad's chores as she could. She cut grass and tried to fix things. Mom was never alone on the weekends. If Dianne was home from school, Laura might go out. Otherwise, she stayed right there with her Mom.

Cheerleader positions came and went, as did friends and opportunities. Not much really mattered. When things began to ease up a bit, Laura went to work at the TV station conducting tours, running the switchboard, and relieving secretaries. She made plans to go off to school, but Dianne made plans to come home. The TV station built a memorial for her Dad and flew flags in his honor. The man from the station that owned the house in the mountains came to Laura's Mom and said that he wanted to help pay for her college expense.

With the blessing of financing, Laura went to college experiencing four of the best years of her life. She continued to work at the TV station on holidays and during the summer. When her benefactor passed away her junior year, she was forced to pay for her senior year herself. Never getting over the loss of her father, she would not dwell on it or let it get her down, but she could not fill the void.

# First Marriage

Laura's first marriage began with the strongest love. It began with undying devotion, physical attraction, matched intellect, and total willingness to uphold all marriage vows. Unfortunately, this was just on Laura's part and not on the part of her husband, Keith.

Keith was a dream-come-true. He was a blind date in college. He was a real charmer. Smart and extremely good looking, he was the perfect size, smell, and taste. He could have been anything he wanted to be and chose to become a salesman. With boyish charm and quick wit to adapt to any situation, he could sell a cat to a rat, and he sold a bill of goods to Laura. Not that at some time he did not love her. He might have, in some little way for some little amount of time. It just was not long enough or strong enough for more than a short haul.

If Laura had looked long and hard enough at the situation, she would have seen the writing on the wall that summer when Keith went behind her back to date her roommate. Instead, she forgave both of them and chalked it up to two people being together in a small town during the summer. What she should have seen was that every female that Laura felt close to, for any reason, became a target for Keith's physical desires.

They were married in February after Laura graduated from college in June. Keith's poor grades had given him the choice of enlist, or be drafted so he had enlisted Obviously lonely and lacking for companionship, Laura not only filled the bill, but footed the bill, too. In her car, they set off to begin their life together in Texas. With six months teaching experience behind her, she was able to land some substituting jobs. They moved into a furnished apartment. Going out for pizza and beer with friends or staying in to read, play cards, and try different foods, it was not a bad time. Once they went to Dallas to visit some friends and once they went to Mexico. Not wanting to make love every night, Keith claimed he did not want it to become a duty. He slowly began chipping away at Laura's self-esteem.

After Texas they were sent to Maryland, where Laura worked in the rental office for their apartment complex. When Keith was sent to Turkey, Laura returned home, where she taught for six months and entertained herself by making Dianne's honeymoon outfits. She paid the bills and waited. Finally, a letter saying that Keith had been transferred to Berlin came the day of her grandmother's funeral—the day after her sister returned from her honeymoon with a broken leg. Dianne had a most unsuccessful snow skiing trip. It was an absolutely wild time. Laura was changing jobs for the third time, trying to pack, selling the car, and doing what she could for her mom and sister.

Berlin was one of the best experiences ever. Laura got a job right away at the American Express office. Whenever she and Keith were off at the same time they went somewhere, sometimes just the two of them, but usually with another couple. They went to Holland, Belgium, Luxembourg, Austria, France, up and down the Rhine River, Barcelona, Madrid, and the French Rivera. They celebrated every holiday with friends. They had fun parties and collected unique memorabilia. Laura learned to cook and speak a little German. They visited all the spots in Berlin, nightlife and daylife, went to CheckPoint Charlie to look over the wall and remembered all the stories of the brave, the pain, the suffering. They ate Curry Wurst from the cart on the street and Chateau Brion at the French Officer's Club. Laura felt truly loved in Berlin. Once, in her presence, Keith actually asked some young military guys not to cuss so much. Perhaps he did love her for a time.

Laura came home a little ahead of Keith. It was time for him to finish his education. Laura found a job and an apartment. Until Keith arrived, she had two jobs, one at school, and one at Belk's. All of her transportation was by bus. It made life a little harder, but more of a challenge. Laura was getting to know some of the people in their apartment complex. It was full of people their age. Donna and Chris lived next-door, super people. Only lacking a year to graduation, Keith arrived about the same time as their new car and immediately enrolled in school.

Keith spent a lot of time in the library. He said he could study better there. Laura worked on the second-hand furniture they had for their apartment. She painted and sewed. When they went out with friends, she still felt very alone. Because she was alone, totally ignored by Keith, the love of her life. Laura never considered herself a beauty queen. She had never been selected as one but she had been nominated for some and served on a few courts and such, but never as a homecoming queen or anything. She stood 5'4", had long brown hair and brown eyes and weighed anywhere from 105 to 109. Whenever she got to 109, Keith would ask why she was getting fat. Most anytime she got ready to go out, his comment was, "Why are you wearing that? Do you really think that looks good?" Laura tried not to notice. Some of the other guys thought she looked fine, and said so. But it was what Keith had to say that mattered.

It was on October 31st that Laura came home from work to find several of the neighborhood guys standing outside Donna's. They stopped her on the way in to tell her that Chris had been killed in a wreck that morning. He had been hit head-on by a drunk driver at 10:30 in the morning. The drunk driver had not been hurt but a passenger in his car was seriously injured.

Laura put her things down and rushed to see Donna. She stayed with her until late that night. It was after she got home that Keith showed up. He immediately went to join the guys.

Over the next two weeks Laura spent as much time as she could with Donna and Jewel, her two-year old. It felt good to be of some support. Actually, Laura did not feel like she had been able to help many people over the last few years. Laura noticed a complete lack of support from Keith. Finally, they had the confrontation.

"What I've noticed over the last two weeks is that Donna has really needed someone to lean on, but when I've needed someone to lean on you have not been here. Are you seeing someone else?"

"Yes. I'm dating the daughter of the secretary at your school."

Shocked, but still capable of speaking, "What's her name?" she replied.

"Melinda"

"Does her mother know? I need to know how to handle things at work?"

"Yes. She thinks it's great. And I'll tell you something else. This Chris that everyone is so sad about was having an affair too."

"Does Donna know?"

"No. Are you going to tell her?"

"No. What would be the point in that?"

"Well, almost every guy I know is having an affair. Even Chuck is having one."

Laura made no further comments on other affairs. It was time to focus on Keith's. "Is there anyway to straighten out this mess?"

"I don't think so."

"Well, then pack what you can carry and get on out of here. You can not take the car. I will not go back to riding the bus so you can screw around."

"Okay"

"Please leave quickly."

He was gone in forty-five minutes. Laura watched the love of her life walk out the door. He turned around long enough to stare at her for a minute, almost as if he had something to say, then turned and walked away. Laura sat in stunned silence. But before the tears welled up too big she picked up the phone and called Jane. "I need to ask you to do me a big favor."

"What is it?"

"I need for you to go to the store, get me a six pack of beer and a pack of cigarettes. I would go myself, but I'm too upset."

"I'll be back as fast as I can. Is Keith gone?"

"Yep, he's moved out."

"I'll hurry. Are you okay?"

"Yeah, I'm fine."

The days were fine, but the nights dragged on and on. Laura had never known such pain. She kept Donna company. She sat at the sewing machine and made ugly clothes to match her mood. She watched her POW get off the plane and mailed him her bracelet. She talked to Chuck, Jane's husband, a little about the separation. It turned out that Chuck was having an affair and so was Jane. Chuck told Laura, "You will be fine. Keith was never there for you and you had to do everything by yourself. The only thing you could have ever gotten from him was a little physical comfort and you will have guys standing in line to provide that for you. In fact, I'm surprised they are not lined up at your door right now. Anything else you need you have the brains to provide for yourself. You have a good job, a good education, and you're a good-looking thing, too. You'll see. You are going to be okay."

Laura still cried herself to sleep most nights, even after drinking a beer or two to calm her down.

She went out once with a friend from school to see a Russian Ballet. It was entertaining and different, but she was very glad to get back home.

She was not ready for male companionship. Her heart was broken. She went home for Thanksgiving and told Dianne about the separation, but no one else.

Her cousin came to town and took her out to dinner. She told him. Her uncle came to town and took her out to dinner. She told him. Finally, she told her Mom.

Keith started calling. He invited her over to see where he was living. He invited her to stay over for the night. She refused. "There are too many people sleeping in this bed already," was her response. Actually, it was just some mats on the floor. Keith had no money for a bed. He borrowed the car one weekend to go for an interview. He graduated and got a job in a small town fifteen miles up the road from Laura's hometown.

He came by one day to see if they could give it another try. He explained that he had even told his new employer that he was married. His affair was over. Now, anyone on the face of the planet would advise Laura not to do this, but they were not the one who was in love with Keith. Why not try to save this marriage? Why not begin again in a new place with new jobs and new friends? Laura accepted the challenge and took Keith back, no questions asked, no discussions. It was a disaster waiting to happen.

Laura left her teaching job in Raleigh and got another one in Caldwell. She knew that she needed to stick to this job because she needed some longevity somewhere. They got an apartment near some friends and started over. Things went well. They moved once to be closer to work and even began looking at houses. They entertained new friends and were entertained in return. Keith was doing well in his salesman position and Laura loved her school and what she was doing. It seemed like things might be okay. Keith played golf with his friends. Laura visited with her family and went to church with them on Sundays.

Laura and Keith bought a house and new furniture for the living room. They joined the Country Club. Life was good. Each summer they spent a week at the beach, with at least three couples, Chris and Joy, Ron and

Amanda, Keith and Laura. If someone could not go, they wouls always find another couple. It was great fun. They pooled their food for breakfast and lunch but hit a nice restaurant for supper. They would dance and sing and enjoy life. Keith continued to play golf and occasionally go out with the boys at night. Sometimes he traveled. Laura played golf and went water skiing with Dianne. When they did, Mom would keep Dianne's boys. When someone mentioned children, Laura would reply, "Keith is not ready."

Keith was not ready for several things. He did not function well when Laura was sick, not that she was sick often. He just seemed obsessed with the golf course. He was usually out of town two nights a week and went out with the guys another night. Sometimes when things got too quiet, Laura would call a friend to see if they could do something. Amanda usually had plans, but others didn't. Laura joined a bridge club in her neighborhood.

Things started to fall apart, again. Keith still made his cutting little remarks about how she dressed or her weight. She had never been in better shape and still held on to 109 pounds. That couldn't be that bad for 5'4'. Occasionally, Laura would notice makeup or lipstick or so she thought on Keith's "away from home" clothes. If she questioned him, he always had just the right answer. Sometimes he had been in a crowd and danced with someone. Sometimes it was her imagination. Laura got so used to his not being at home that the sound of the garage door opening and closing did not even wake her.

Ron and Amanda separated. Keith and Laura helped them move. Amanda moved into a nice apartment. Sometimes Laura felt sorry for her and sometimes she envied her. She was so pretty and slim, had a nice job, and had plenty of dates. Laura helped her as much as possible and occasionally they went places together.

Laura suggested that she and Keith go to a marriage counselor before their marriage met with the same fate. Keith agreed, but was horrible.

They went together and then they went separately. When Laura went back for another private session, the counselor told her, "You husband will not admit to having an affair, but I'm convinced that he is. He will not leave you because you are too good and you are too good to him. I do not see your marriage getting better; I see it getting worse. The best thing you can do for yourself is to leave or find someway to make him leave and then you need to find someone for yourself."

Laura was devastated. What was all this? Marriage counselors were suppose to make things work, not tell you to separate. Holy cow!

A week passed before Laura could discuss the situation with Keith. When she finally got up the nerve they were standing in the garage. She spilled the beans on the counselor and waited for Keith's reply. This was what she heard. "Laura, I am not good to you. I never have been. I might be someday, but it will probably be a long time from now. You are a good person. You deserve someone who will be good to you. I don't think that someone is me. I'm not saying that I don't love you. I do love you, but I love you more like a sister than a wife."

Well, what do you say to that? Nothing. You go inside and find something to do quickly while you look at things from your new perspective.

A few Saturdays later Keith left to play golf and Laura sat in the den pondering her situation. Keith called after a few hours to say that he wasn't coming home. He was going to Don's. It looked like Keith would be gone until sometime Sunday morning. Laura thought about her life and the advice she had gotten, picked up the phone and called Don. Don told her that Keith had not gotten there yet. "Well, that's fine. When he gets there, y'all help him out some; maybe you can find him a place to stay. Please tell him that he has lost his wife and he needs to come get his stuff."

Keith was home in no time. "Are you sure about this?" was the question.

"Yes, I'm very sure. I've had plenty of time to think."

"I'll go if you really want me to."

"I want you to. Are you going now?"

"Yes, I guess I will."

"Good. Please hurry." And that was it. Laura was almost relieved. If she had been entirely sure of her future, she would have been completely at ease. This was not nearly as painful as the first time. In fact, Laura was not even concerned enough to call anyone for moral support.

Keith moved in with Don, and Laura started working on her master's degree. She considered selling the house, but decided to wait a few months. Sometimes she did things with friends, and she did a lot with family. A neighbor formally introduced her to Scott, the stud that lived down the street. He walked her home and told her that he did not like to see marriages fall apart, but he had wanted to meet her for a long time. Life was pretty interesting.

She saw Amanda on campus every now and then. They would eat out some. Laura was beginning to feel more confident in herself. Scott called often and they finally agreed to see each other.

Their first date was really nice because he was very much the gentleman. He gave her the slightest little kiss at the front door and took his exit. Laura fairly floated to the bedroom where much to her surprise—Keith came walking out of the closet.

"What the hell are you doing in this house?" was Laura retort once she stopped herself from letting go with a scream. "How dare you hide in this house like this! Are you crazy? How did you know I had a date? How did you know I wouldn't shoot you? What if we had come in here and gone to bed?" She was furious.

"I'm sorry. I just needed to talk to you. I know I was taking a chance on getting shot, but I didn't think that Scott would be coming in. I think I know you well enough that I was safe on that. I just want to talk to you. I want to come back. I want us to work things out. I don't know what's wrong with me, but I would like to have you in my life. I know I deserve it for you to start dating someone else, but I'm here to try to talk you out of it. I want you to be with me."

Laura could not believe her ears. What chaos and confusion, what a bag of mixed emotions this conversation in this place at this hour of the morning was producing. She listened to Keith for two hours. Finally, she said, "You will have to leave now. I'm not making any decisions now; I'm too confused. You will have to give me some time, some time for thinking and some time for getting myself together, and I don't mean 24 hours, maybe 24 days."

"Whatever it takes."

"Okay, you need to go now. Where is your car? It's almost daylight. I'll do some thinking and give you a call."

"Okay, that's all I can ask. I'm sorry for scaring you." And he left.

After making sure the doors were secured a little better, Laura crawled in bed and snuggled down in the covers. What a trip. She decided to save it until tomorrow and drifted off to sleep.

Laura was not going to make a hasty decision. Her mind would not tolerate it. She really missed Keith, but she was not sure that her love was as strong as it once was. There had been too much hurt. Other people, Amanda, Scott, and family, were cautioning her to be careful. Had he changed or was he just after what he didn't have. It was impossible to tell. Maybe time would reveal something. She really liked Scott, but did she still love Keith? Who was Keith anyway? Yet, to save a marriage, it was okay to make sacrifices.

Keith kept calling. He showed up at school. He invited her on trips. He promised his undying love while seducing her.

Laura figured that if she were sleeping with her husband, she could not date someone else and ended the relationship with Scott. He seemed to understand, wished her the best, and said that he would be around if she needed him.

Life went well with Keith for a few months, and then Laura noticed that some things were slipping again. The golf continued. The parties continued. The physical relationship was satisfactory, but there were stretches when some mighty fine sex should have occurred and it did not. Once Keith said that she was the very best. Laura secretly wondered to whom she was being compared. Occasionally, Keith was out of town, but not often.

Then one night it happened. Keith was out of town and Laura went to pick up something for supper. This was a very rare occasion because normally she just ate cereal or leftovers. On this particular night, she passed Keith's car out on the highway. When she got home she waited to see when he would return. Nothing. She called his office the next day and asked why he was still in town so late, had he forgotten something? No, she was told. She did not see him. It was her imagination. Right, in every small town there are hundreds of silver 240z's with the same license number and good-looking brown-haired men driving them. Now Laura was back on guard.

A few weeks later Laura opened the phone bill. There were five or six calls on it to Amanda from out-of-town. Laura walked around the block five times holding the phone bill. "What would be the explanation for this?" Laura wondered and prayed for the best.

Then she showed Keith the bill. "What? Let me see?" Upon careful examination Keith said, "Oh, I know what this was about. I have talked to her several times. Sometimes about us and sometimes about guys she's dating. She just always wanted someone to talk to. I honestly didn't think you would mind if I talked to her. You two are very good friends." Laura felt guilty for suspecting Amanda. She had been a lot of comfort for a long time because Ron had not treated Amanda very well during their marriage, either.

Keith and Laura had been married more than eight years. The first two years in Texas and Berlin had been wonderful times. They had experienced so much and seen enough to last a lifetime; Mexico, deserts, amusement parks, Texas steaks, The Alamo, tulips and windmills in

Holland, Bull fights in Madrid, beer, Cathedrals, the aqua-colored water of the Mediterranean in Nice, Amsterdam, bridges in Cologne, lace in Belgium, peach wine in France, castles on the Rhine river, Von Lugwig's model for Disneyland, Frankfort, Berlin, Dachou, Innsbruck, and all the sights and sounds along the way. Keith's stepfather passed away and nephews were born. Friends had been plentiful. Successes had been plentiful. But as time passed things grew worse.

Laura could not put her finger on what was wrong. She felt like excess baggage, and it wasn't a pleasant feeling. She was working on her master's degree, but at the moment she did not feel she could support herself on her salary, at least not in the new house. She took home $465 and the house payment was $340. That did not leave much room for food and repairs or utility bills. Was it worth it or would it be better to cut your losses? Where was her gumption? She would have never been like this in college. Had Keith damaged her self-esteem that badly? He had not affected her job because he could not get to it, but he had managed to make her feel pretty low on every other scale. How long would it take to repair the damage and could she do it and stay married to him?

The Christian side of Laura was also empowering her. One of the few acceptable reasons for divorce was fornication, if she remembered correctly. Well, Melinda took care of that and whatever was going on now would finish it off. Laura was still holding her weight at 109 pounds, sometimes less, but for some reason Keith still considered her fat. Whoever this someone is that she was competing with was smaller, not necessarily slimmer, but smaller-framed for sure. Was she smart or just good in bed? Who knows? Somebody knew, that's a given.

One evening Keith came home to find Laura packing the car. "What are you doing?"

"I'm leaving and I'm taking the "Z""

"Can we discuss this?"

"No, it won't do any good. My mind is made up. I'm tired of the way things are going, and I just need to leave. We can talk about selling the house or whatever later. Right now, I just have to get out of here." She packed the car as full as she could. She got Bo Jangles, the black lab from the dog lot, and off she went.

Mom was surprised but very glad to see her.

Laura spent two or three weeks getting herself together. She saw an attorney, went to work, and to school. She was headed into the final stretch for her master's and she would be through in another year. She took care of Bo Jangles, what a great friend. Mom did not allow dogs in the house so she spent hours on the porch being comforted by a Labrador. She talked to some friends at school, but mostly she talked to her mother and sister. She got up the nerve to call Scott. Yes, he would love to see her. Could he take her to dinner some night next week? Sure.

Keith and Laura's anniversary arrived. He sent two dozen roses to her at work. "What the hell is this?" was her question to one of her good teacher buddies. Actually, she and Di were getting pretty close. Di had the same name as her sister and the same china pattern as herself. That should tell you something. Di had good family ties and her father was a preacher. "Do you know," she said to Di, "that in the eight years we were married, Keith never sent me flowers? Do you know that in eight years we never spent an anniversary alone? We always had to have company or go somewhere with someone. Now we have flowers. How touching."

"When they arrived, we were surprised that they were for you. We thought that they were Mildred's because today is her birthday."

"Is Mildred still here?"

"I think she is in the cafeteria."

"Okay, let's change this card and send them to her. I can't stand to look at these things." And Di delivered the flowers to Mildred. The saying about garbage and gold is true.

Laura went to the beach for a weekend with Amanda. They discussed the ups and downs of being single. Laura called Scott. Amanda called whoever.

Scott put Laura on a pedestal. Laura did not know at the time that pedestals could also be dangerous. He was kind, told her she was pretty, opened doors, and took her out to dinner. Gorgeous, fun, and rich, he had brothers and a nice family. All Laura needed was that final break with Keith and it was not long in coming.

Scott would tell her if he noticed strange comings and goings at her ex-home. He said he noticed a female in a red sports car checking out the estate once. Was that a real estate agent, maybe? No, nothing was for sale. In fact, Laura was sending Keith the money to make the house payment. He was paying the other bills. Laura did not know of anyone who drove a red sports car, must be a new girl in town.

One evening Scott asked if he could come over. This was unusual because they usually made their plans well in advance. He said he needed to talk to her. So they talked. And the conversation went like this. "Laura, I saw something today that I know is going to upset you. It would upset anyone. Are you ready?"

"Well, I'm as ready as I'll ever be."

"For awhile now Keith has been taking someone to your house. I wasn't sure who it was for a long time. Once I passed them on the street and this girl actually ducked her head. That made me real curious because there was no reason for her to duck unless I knew her. I saw her last night. It was Amanda. I made sure because I could not let you know if there was any doubt in my mind. It was Amanda. Keith has been seeing Amanda for God only knows how long. I hate to tell you. You probably will never want to see me again for letting you know, but I had too. Amanda has helped herself to Keith and given you self-serving advice since the beginning. What can I do? Do you want me to leave?"

"When I get real upset in a few minutes you will need to leave. Before I absorb all this I need to thank you for letting me know. I also need to know if you will come back tomorrow night and take me out to dinner."

"Of course I will. Can I do anything now?"

"No, I need 24 hours. Oh, yes, there is one thing."

"What is it?"

"Will you please give me a hug?"

As the magnitude of what Laura had heard began to sink in, Laura felt herself grow weaker. She felt herself sinking into a pit that was very dark and very deep. She went to the phone and called Keith. "Are you seeing Amanda?" She asked in a very calm voice. She knew that she was sinking too fast to be able to waste energy on screaming and shouting and throwing things around.

"Yes."

"When did you start seeing her?"

"Not long after we moved here, so I guess it's been about four years. I was surprised you never figured it out."

"We went on vacations together. Are you in love with her and are you going to marry her?"

"No. I'm not in love with her and I'm not going to marry her. In fact, I'm not going to be seeing her anymore. I was hoping we could work something out for us."

"I don't think so. I don't know who you are."

"Uh, Laura, there is one thing. We talked about telling you, but Amanda did not want you to know. She really loves you and she wanted you to be friends."

"Some friend. Goodbye now."

Laura dialed Amanda's number extra fast. "Hey, Amanda, it's Laura."

"How are you doing? I've been meaning to call."

"Amanda, have you been sleeping with Keith?"

Short pause to suck in breath, then "Yes, I have. I have been meaning to tell you, but I didn't want to hurt you."

"You have been meaning to tell me for four years?"

"Yes, I have. I really like you, Laura. I'm really sorry I hurt you. I'm really sorry."

"Yes, you are sorry. You are a sorry excuse for a friend and you are a very sorry excuse for a church secretary."

"Are you going to tell anyone?"

"I'm going to tell everyone I know so they can protect themselves from your friendship. I have to go now. Goodbye."

It would be years before Laura learned that anything could be more painful than what she was experiencing. It was actually worse than death because it was the death of two people. It was complete vaporization of two people that she once thought would be in her life forever. It was total and complete destruction. She cried some, but mostly she was too dumbstruck to do much crying. It was like stepping into an abyss of apathy. Laura continued to function at work. She went to church and fought being bitter or feeling sorry for herself. She quit sending Keith money for the house payment. She spent very healing time with her nephews, Kevin and Brad. They did not try to discuss Keith with her because they were too young. They were innocent and full of love and play, just what the doctor ordered for Laura.

Keith showed up at school and asked Laura to please come by the house. He wanted to discuss their situation. She went, not really knowing why. Keith sat on one side of the bar and she stood on the other. It should have been more than obvious that their situation was hopeless. Laura understood this completely, which enabled her to carry on a conversation. Keith seemed to think that as long as he was not seeing Amanda that they still had a chance to work things out. Unfortunately, relationships can suffer permanent damage. Enough permanent damage that the relationship can not be repaired. Laura had learned this. She had loved Keith more than life itself and now she had absolutely no feelings for or against him. Sure, she would be sorry if he got run over by a pick-up truck or bus or something, because, after all, he was a human being, but she just had no more emotion for him, good or bad. Total apathy, or so she thought. She just had one more minor phase to go through. Call it anger.

At the house she gathered the nerve to ask Keith if he could explain why he had affairs. She wanted to know if it were her fault so maybe she could correct whatever it was that she was doing wrong. He replied, "Laura, you are the most perfect woman I have ever known, so when I meet any other woman, I look to find their best talent. I look for what they do best. It doesn't matter if it's their cooking, talking, job, typing, whatever. Then I compare them to you, just in that one area. If they do that one thing better than you do, then I try to sleep with them." What that meant to Laura was that he was going to sleep with everyone. No wonder she couldn't compete with this. It was impossible. She asked him to repeat what he said. Then she said, "So at some time or the other I'm suppose to compete with someone who dances better, someone else who sings better, someone else who is smarter, someone else who is better in bed, someone else who cooks better?"

"Yes, I guess so. But it's hard to find those people. You are very good in bed. You are beautiful. You are smart. You cook really great. You do most things better than anybody. So I really have to look to find someone who does something better than you."

"But, that's a lot of fun, the looking and all, is that right?"

"Yeah, that's the best part."

Laura said, "Excuse me, I need to use the restroom," and entered the small bathroom off the hall. She stood looking in the mirror for a long minute and then it happened. She picked up a bottle of cologne off the back of the commode and sent it crashing to the floor. She said not a word. Keith came running to the door and said, "Are you okay?"

Laura replied, "Yes, I'm fine. I'll be out in a minute." She grabbed another bottle and threw it on the floor. She threw all the bottles on the floor. She grabbed medicine from the cabinet and let fly with them. She aimed at the tub walls so the smashed bottles and contents could run down the sides and settle at the bottom. What a show! What a superb art show!

Keith was pounding on the door, "What are you doing? Are you okay? Please come out of there!" He was in a total panic.

Laura broke everything she could and emptied everything else. It was great. What a release! When everything she could get her hands on was smashed and broken, Laura exited the bathroom. Keith was standing by the door.

"Are you okay? Good Lord, look at this mess! Look at what you did! There's broken glass all over the floor!"

"Yeah, I know. It felt real good. I have to go now." She turned and walked out the door.

The next few months progressed fairly calmly. Laura continued to see Scott. His attentiveness made her feel good about herself.

Laura continued in school. Hopefully, she would have her master's someday. It was a real struggle with all this other mess going on.

Dianne still came to her rescue. They played par-three golf on Saturdays and went water skiing on Thursdays.

Once during the summer, Laura got pretty sick. It was strept throat or something. Scott was outside playing with Bo Jangles when Laura decided to take her temperature. It was 104. Her Mom was taking a nap. When you have suffered through people running away from you because you are sick, it's hard to know what to do when you can't stand up. Laura knocked as loudly as possible on the window to get Scott's attention without waking up Mom. After what seem like an eternity he came in the back door. When he got to the living room Laura whispered, "Something is wrong and I don't know what to do."

"I can see that something is wrong, what is it and what can I do?"

"My temperature is 104. I don't want to wake up Mom and I don't want to try to find a doctor on Sunday. Will you try to help me get this temperature down?"

"Hell, yes. What do you want me to do?"

"First get me some aspirin before I get sick on my stomach."

"Okay, be right back." And he was. "Here, take these and sip on this ice water. I'm going to get a wash rag and some alcohol." For the next 45 minutes Scott gave Laura a soothing, cooling alcohol rub. Laura had never experienced such kindness. By the time Mom woke up, the temperature was down and Laura felt much better. She knew to see the doctor tomorrow for a prescription and not to let too much time lapse between aspirins. Scott left Laura in the more than capable hands of Mom.

Keith and Laura tried to settle their estate. It went back and forth between attorneys for awhile. Laura received advice like, "Well, we could really burn this guy if it wasn't for Amanda pretending to be you friend. Unfortunately, she knows you are seeing Scott and there is no telling what she might say or do. My suggestion is that you keep the house and let Keith pay the few bills you have. If you can't make the house payment, then sell the house. You should be fine. Sometimes the people that you are a best friend to, are not your best friend. They are someone else's. Anyway, don't send Keith any more money for the house payment. There's no sense in pouring any more water down that empty well." No shit.

Laura asked Keith if he would give her $75 a month to help with the house payment for six months. After that time, if she worked very hard, she would either have her master's or she would sell the house. Mom and Laura were both real estate brokers so there shouldn't be much of a problem showing and selling the house. Keith agreed to do this, but only for six months, after that any money would have to be paid back when the house was sold. Laura thought, "There are names for people like this, its called "Son of a Bitch'." Then Keith convinced Laura of his true character with this line, "Laura, I have been really bad to you. I have treated you simply awful. I have been so bad to you that no amount of money in this wide world could ever make up for what I have done to you. There is nothing I could ever do to make all this up to you, so I'm not going to do anything. Every dime you get from me you will have to fight for."

And she did. And she did. She ended up with a 240z in pretty good condition, a fairly new house, and a great dog. What was missing in the way of house furnishings could be fixed in some way. Accepting another challenge, she used the old furniture from Raleigh for the living room and added a tea crate from Taiwan for an end table. She repainted and rearranged until she had something workable. She covered a whole wall with different sized and types of envelopes containing dried flowers. It was strange, but true.

Independence set in. She allowed Scott to put her on a pedestal, she spent a lot of time with her family, and she worked hard on her masters. Then it was the winter at the end of the six month $75 period. Laura still took home $485 a month and had the house payment of $340. She had $145 to cover food, electricity, heat, water, insurance, food, clothes, repairs, medical and gifts. She took on a tutoring job for $6 an hour. She put this money aside for Christmas. The first $6 was for cards and each $6 after that bought a gift until she had everyone covered. Lots of people got cross-stitch that year. Her mother and sister got reversible coats, which Laura made. She made herself one, too. To save on electricity she closed off the living room and two bedrooms, actually Laura referred to them as the sewing room and the study since they did not contain beds. She ate her breakfast and lunch at school. Lunch became her main meal of the day. If Scott took her out to eat, she took a doggie bag for the next night. She managed to pay her bills, but she wore sandals with socks all winter because she could not afford shoes. Scott asked what she would do with $100 if she had it. She said she would pay her part of the river cabin taxes and spend the rest on his Christmas present. He gave it to her. She spent it exactly like she said. He said he couldn't believe that she didn't do something for herself. She replied, "I did. I am."

Keith started calling. He asked to meet her for dinner. Fool that she was, she went, mostly out of curiosity. Keith sat in the restaurant. He was all humble and nice and gave the most wonderful speech about how much he loved her. He had changed. He wanted nothing more than to make her happy for the rest of her life. There would not be any other women. He would spend his time with her and would see to it that she could continue to enjoy the river cabin. He would do anything she wanted if she would just let him come home.

Laura listened to him for an hour or so, and then she said, "No. I do not want you back."

Keith argued that if she was saying no because of Scott, he, Keith, was a much better deal.

Laura said, "Scott has nothing to do with this, this is between you and me and the answer is 'no'."

Keith stared at her for a long time. It was almost the look he had when he paused that moment before walking out the door in Raleigh. Finally he spoke, "I know I deserve this. But for the life of me, I can't believe that I am asking you to do something and you are telling me, 'no'."

"Well, I am. You should try to get used to it." The evening ended quickly. Jimmy and Don and their current ladies came in the door. "What are they doing here?"

"They are here to help us celebrate our getting back together."

"What? You had the nerve to plan that? Well, I hope you think of something good to tell them because I'm gone."

Basically, that was the end of Keith. Laura tried not to spend much time dwelling on him and he was only a topic for conversation when someone else brought him up. She began the life-long process of repairing her self-esteem. Sometimes it takes a lifetime because the hurt is so deep and that is okay. Pick who you can share your hurts with carefully and don't go blabbing and blubbering to just anyone. Take care of yourself. Let the Lord take care of you, too.

# Fisticuff

Laura survived the winter. She continued her math courses and enjoyed her nephews. Sometimes they would spend the night with her. Her relationship with Scott grew a little more serious and there was talk of rings and things. Scott had a ring made out of his fraternity pin and gave it to Laura. They danced and played. He bought a house on the next street, within walking distance to her house. Someone at work asked Laura if Scott had a bad temper because they had heard of that from somewhere. Laura replied, "Not that I know of. I haven't seen it, but I'll be on the lookout." Actually, she could remember several times. Once he had picked her up and carried her back into his apartment so they could finish a discussion, but Laura was under the impression that he was just fooling around. She had to return to the parking lot the next day to hunt for the things that had fallen from her purse. The other was a comment Scott had made once about being too hard on his ex-wife and his son. And then there was the time they went out to eat and Scott got upset because she was gazing at the stained glass window behind him. He thought she was looking at a table of men, so he told her she should look at her food or look at him. Not a real good thing to say to Miss Independence. She should have seen it coming.

Instead, she put her house on the market. It did not sell and after six months there had only been one offer. Then Laura got a tax return of $900. Amazing! She put $300 aside for car expense, $300 for vacation, and $300 for emergencies. She still did not buy shoes because the weather was getting warmer and sandals were okay. She decided to take the house off the market and try to make it through another year. She studied like mad. She was taking a programming course and a math course. Scott helped her by calling out questions for her orals. For a break from studying she cut grass or went water skiing with Dianne.

By the middle of August she had passed her orals. It would be the first of October before she would see a change in her salary. She could hardly wait. She really had no idea what her new pay would be, but she knew that if she was going to be able to keep the house she had to reach $620 a month.

Scott's birthday was August 19th. He was very much a Leo. He did not like sweets so Laura baked him a caraway seed rye bread cake with cream cheese icing. She had a couple of bottles of red wine. Scott got incredibly drunk and ruined the whole evening with some silly argument. Laura locked herself in the bathroom and waited for him to go home. What a bad birthday party! He came over the next morning to apologize and they made up just fine.

Then it happened. It was a very pleasant end of August evening, just the type that calls out for a neighborhood pool party. So even with the sprained ankle acquired when cutting grass, Laura grabbed Scott and made a beeline for the fun, food, and the sounds of a live band. It promised to be another chance for a single girl in her thirties to enjoy her blessings. It isn't easy to dance with a sprained ankle, so luckily the evening evolved into conversation with good friends.

There developed somewhat of a verbal sparring match between Scott and Matt. Laura wasn't really paying too much attention and only commented briefly that most people do the best they can most of the time. She had no idea that she had crossed any line or stepped into a death abyss.

As the evening was ending and Scott and Laura walked across the street and up the hill to her house. Scott said, "I don't appreciate your taking Matt's side of things at the pool."

"What? I didn't mean to take sides. I just think most people try hard. I'm sorry if it sounded different. I certainly did not mean to take sides with anyone." As they closed the front door behind them, Scott took Laura's hand and led her down the hall to the bedroom. She was traveling a little fast for her ankle, but the bedroom had never proved to be an unpleasant place.

Once through the bedroom door Scott turned and with the quickest of moves, knocked the hell out of Laura's face. She was too stunned to think. She stammered, "You hit me. You hit me? You hit me!" She realized a little something else upon looking in the mirror "You cut my tongue. You cut my tongue!" Her lack of experience with domestic violence left her totally unprepared for the rest of the evening. Scott was now standing behind her pointing the small pistol he had given to her for protection. "Are you going to shoot me?" He continued to point the gun. "Are you going to shoot me?" was all she could manage to say. She stood frozen.

Scott took the gun and placed it in her hand. "You have a chance to shoot me now, if you want to." Well, hell no, Laura did not want to shoot anyone. She just wanted the evening over with and she wanted her face and mouth to stop hurting. If she had been more adept at violence, she might have fired a few shots. Next time, she would. Right now, she was in a place she had never been and pretty much in a total panic.

"No, I don't want to shoot you." was her reply.

With that, Scott grabbed the gun and the rest of the evening began. He dragged Laura, now kicking and screaming, down the hall and threw her onto the kitchen floor. At once he was on top of her smashing his hand into her face. Then, as suddenly as it began, it was over. Scott got up, went to the bar, sat down and had himself a smoke. Laura was trying to get herself together when suddenly Scott was on her again, slamming his hand across her face. Then he would stop and smoke. This went on and on. At one point, Laura crawled across the kitchen floor and was leaning against the wall. When Scott began to drag her back across the floor, she grabbed the curtains to hold her place. The rod bent and finally pulled free of the wall before she let go. The blows were much the same. Why was this happening? What was going to make it stop? Then it stopped. Scott went for another smoke. This will go on until I'm dead. Laura was sure of that. Laura realized that she was going to have to think. Don't try the "hug the wall and hold on to the curtains" thing, again. It did no good. Think. Look for another plan. Thoughts were gathering in her head. She looked around. There was a poker by the fireplace. She had to make a decision. Pick up the poker or head for the door. Was the door locked? If it was, she had no chance. Not a good chance anyway, on a bad foot. But if she chose the poker, he'd probably kill her with it.

Laura waited for Scott to pick up his cigarette. In a minute Scott took a big drag. With the smoke going in, he'd have to exhale and breathe again before he reacted. Laura dashed, maybe flew, to the door, grabbed the knob, and it turned! She was out the door but she could hear Scott close on her heels!

She ran like the wind to the neighbor's next door. As she climbed the steps she thought, 'I hate to do this to you, Chip, but here goes!' And as her fists pounded on the front door she screamed, "Chip, its Laura! Please help me! Please let me in! Please help me!"

There was no answer. Laura realized that no on was home at the same time she heard the footsteps behind her. When she turned around she saw three Scotts headed towards her. What she heard was "Laura, it's Tom Rhodes, it's Tom Rhodes, it's Tom Rhodes!" It was not Scott. It was Tom, Bob, and Matt. These were good friends who had stayed behind after the pool party to clean up. Laura collapsed on the steps.

She told her story quickly and Bob and Matt took off to find Scott. Tom stayed with Laura. After a bit, they returned. They had found Scott sitting on the front steps of Laura's house, holding the gun, and saying, "I wasn't going to shoot her. I wasn't going to shoot her." They took the gun and took him home.

The group decided that it would be best for Laura to spend the night at Matt and Emily's house and they escorted her there. Emily listened to the tale of horror and did what she could for Laura's bruises and nerves. Not much could be done for her emotions, but a good night's sleep in a safe place began the healing process. Yes, a good night's sleep in a safe place will begin the healing process.

Laura went to Chris and Joy's the next morning. With rumors flying all over the neighborhood, she had a couple of calls from people who were willing to deal with Scott, but she refused. Joy stayed with her the whole day, listening and trying to ease her pain. They tried to plan for the future. Chris changed every lock on every door at Laura's house. She went home before bedtime with plans, should the plans be necessary, for any emergencies. She thanked the Lord that she was alive.

Labor Day weekend, she went to the river with her Mom, and Dianne's family joined them. She could always relax and get her thoughts together at the river. There was good food and fun and family. There was nothing to compare with the sunset at the river. Even with all the happiness, she still had to keep makeup on her face to hide the bruises.

Later she got her back tooth fixed and talked to the doctor about her elbow. She had a chipped bone but the doctor said it would heal on its own.

When school started the next week Laura had a terrible time writing lesson plans. In fact, it was the first time in her ten years of teaching that she started off the year with really bad plans. She was sure it would take her until Thanksgiving to make this up to her students. She was having trouble making any plans at all for anything. Mostly, she just drifted. One day she decided to make a list of the men she felt she would feel safe with. There were only three, a principal from another school system who was out because he was married. She would not consider seeing a married man. Even if it were not one of the "Big Ten", Laura's nickname for the Ten Commandments, the hurt from Keith would be enough for her never to inflict that pain on someone else. The other two were high school sweethearts. One was now a college graduate; the other was a dropout who played a guitar. Her decision was which one to call first.

# Between

Laura found Paul. He was still gorgeous. Bat Masterson, James Garner, and Walter Mathou with a sense of humor was like Johnny Carson, all rolled into one. His aqua-blue eyes reminded Laura of the pictures of the Caribbean and there was no doubt that you could dive in them and swim around. Long black eyelashes protected them. When you saw these eyelashes from the side, they had to carry on for at least an inch. Paul was her hero. He was a music man. He would play his "six string" and sing to her for hours. He liked her hair. He liked her touch and she liked his. There was an outside chance that he was the real love of her life rather than Keith. She had never forgotten him from high school. Building her up, he restored much of Laura's self-esteem. Enough to make her write poems.

Laura knew not to get too close, because it was not to last. Paul was a vagabond. So when the seasons changed and Paul began making his plans to spend the winter in Florida, Laura steadied herself for the coming disaster. They made it through Christmas. Laura bought Neil Diamond tickets as a present and Paul gave her a double album with the same songs.

In January he left for Florida. They kept in touch a little, but not much. Both moved on to other things. For Laura, this was as difficult a separation as the one she had experienced with Keith. But she knew that the two of them would never make it because they were too different. She had three degrees more than Paul. He was music; she was math. He was a vagabond; she was a schoolteacher. Laura would love Paul forever and would always welcome a chance to see him. Until she died she would still look for his name on music covers and hope to catch him in a live performance. He gave her back her life and she would be eternally grateful.

It would be four months before Laura could even consider dating anyone. When she did, it went nowhere. Finally, she contacted the other name on her list. Although, they had some fun, she felt nothing. It was as if he was still in college doing college things and she was way on down the road. Through him, however, she did meet some other people and became reacquainted with some high school friends, including Alex, that she dated for six months, or so. Again, nothing would come of love in this in between time in Laura's life.

# Time Out for God

Laura had spent several years in the classroom when she ran across a lesson on the second dimension. It was extremely interesting in that everything in the second dimension must be flat due to having only length and width. She decided to present a dimension study to her students. As it was not part of the tested curriculum, it would have to fall on a day when attendance was not good or everything else had been covered. Now, the first dimension was just length, just a straight line going somewhere. Whether it went around the earth or out into space depended on how you defined your geometry. This would come up in class to produce a good discussion. In a three-dimensional world you couldn't see this line because it had no width or height. It could only be imagined. The second dimension had another feature called width. It had to be at right angles with length. These two together would produce a plane, often illustrated by a piece of paper or a parallelogram drawn on a sheet of paper. The best illustration Laura knew of was the Colgate invisible shield, but her students were too young to remember the commercial. So this lesson, newly discovered, made things easier to see. It was about a housing plan for flat people. What you had to work with was getting around. You could not stack anything because there was no height and you could not plan to crawl over anything either. You could only pass another person by going completely around so you needed to watch your doors and inside spaces very carefully. What a fun day this would be.

You also had to be ready to discuss the third and fourth dimensions. The third was the easiest because everyone was most familiar with it. It had three dimensions, length, width, and height, all perpendicular to each other. We lived in it. We could understand it. We could also understand that, just like the second dimension, you could not go through another person or object; you had to go around or over. The fourth dimension was something of a completely different nature. Oh, it had the length, width, height thing and all at right angles to each other, but it also had another unit and it had to be at right angles with the other three. To make matters worse, you could not visualize this in a three-dimensional world. You could not see it any more than you could one or two dimensions, but it was more difficult because you didn't even have good examples like a line or a sheet of paper.

Laura had read several stories to her classes on the fourth dimension trying to get them to think. One in particular told of a doctor who discovered the secret to the fourth dimension and would go there to perform surgeries on three-dimensional patients. Because he was free to move about without being detected, he could actually enter a patient's body and perform the operation without having to cut open the patient. It also described the way he looked coming and going to the fourth dimension. You would only see the part of his body that was actually in the third dimension. It would increase or decrease in completeness as he came and went. It had a tendency to be gross but students ate it up.

Another phenomenon to keep in mind was that the second dimension could contain the first, the third contain the second, and the fourth contain the third. Each higher dimension could directly influence a lower dimension without the lower dimension being totally aware of what was taking place. They should be able to sense that there was something more powerful messing with them even if they could not see it, just as we sometimes sense that there is something affecting our universe that we cannot see. For example, if you took a three-dimensional object, say a pencil, and stuck it through a two-dimensional space, say a sheet of paper. What would the people living in the two-dimensional world see? They would first see a small dot, which would increase in size. Then a hole would actually appear in their world. It might even have a yellow ring around it as the size stabilized. Then a flash of gold and pink might appear around the edge as the metal ring and eraser went through, but the hole would remain. Would they call this a black hole? It would certainly cause much discussion as to its meaning.

Laura was prepared to answer as many questions as possible. She would be asked if time was the fourth dimension and if the wind was the fourth dimension. She figured the wind to be a product of the third dimension, but time was tricky. She just could not see time being that powerful. It was certainly something that existed and acted without control. But Laura felt that time was basic to all dimensions. In fact, it was her guess that time might actually be the first dimension, actually present first and used in all dimensions as the aging process occurred. So it could be that we were living in the fourth dimension and looking for the fifth.

What impressed Laura the most was this popping in and out of the third dimension. It could go a long way in explaining strange appearances and even apparitions. If the fourth dimension were God, or heaven, it would explain the strange comings and goings of spirits and angels. It would certainly help explain some of the miracles, some of the unexplained healings. As Laura thought more about this it seemed to help with the idea of the Holy Spirit living in us, the spirit that grows stronger as we grow closer to God and communicate through prayer. Laura could find no real fault with her theory. In fact, it made her feel peaceful just to think about it. So, at death, this Holy Spirit, this soul, could transcend into the next dimension. No fuss. No hassle. Communication had already been established by belief.

This was not an idea that could be discussed in class, but it sure could be discussed among her friends. Laura just needed to find someone that would take the time to understand the math and examine the religious aspects. People would probably think she was crazy, but it certainly would not be the first time. She had never seen any real conflict with the Bible and science. In her poor feeble mind she could tie together the math/science and the theology courses just fine.

Laura's first true religious experience had occurred when she was nine. Up to that time she had done the usual for a southern Christian family. She had been to Sunday school and church on a regular basis. Her mom and dad were both involved in the Sunday school program. She was in the choir and attended Vacation Bible School. They also went to Wednesday night supper about once a month. They had a blessing before meals and a prayer at bedtime. Religious holidays were faithfully kept. It was a very pleasant situation. It was just done; no screaming and shouting, no TV evangelists, just stable, southern fried religion.

At the age of nine, Laura had never noticed religion being put to a test. She was totally unaware of any struggle an adult might be having with any demons. Only on rare occasions did she hear of really bad things happening. She knew she had scared her family really bad the day she got lost coming home from school, but she had no idea of the evils that could have befallen her. This was the setting when she could not find her tea set.

The tea set was a small plastic collection of cups and plates and other containers for the most delicate of parties. The cups were only about 1/2 inch high and wide. They were all contained in a blue and white doll hatbox that measured 4 inches in diameter and 2 inches high. Laura had looked all through her closet, under her bed, in her special "hiding" corner, everywhere she could imagine. Soon the search had spread throughout the house, covering kitchen, den, and living room. Laura found herself in her mom's bedroom in total distress.

At that point Laura got down on her knees and prayed to the Lord, "Dear God, I know I'm not suppose to pray for selfish things, but is there any way You can help me find my tea set? I've looked everywhere I can and I just can't find it. Please help me. In Jesus' name. Amen."

Laura stood up and felt the calm descend. What's more, she felt someone telling her to go to her room. She did. The same sensation said to go to her closet. She did. Then she heard, "Look down to the left corner." There it was. Laura sat on the floor in amazement. Did what just happened really happen? How could this be? She was overjoyed that the Lord had heard her prayer. As she picked up the tea set, she knew this was something she would never forget, if she lived 100 years.

So for the rest of her life, no matter how far she strayed from formal religion or what wild "sixties" ideas came and went or strange preachers preaching strange ideas, Laura had a strong religious background, a background that let her know that prayers would be answered. She could never deny the Lord or His Power and Compassion. The foundation was set.

# Second Marriage

Jeff and Laura were married the Saturday before Easter. They had met two years before when Laura had gone to the beach for four days with her running buddies, Jayne, Melanie, and Lucy. It was the third day at the beach and although the other ladies had danced and met people, Laura just seemed to sit and watch the rest of the world go by. She was all dolled up but was she really ready? On that last night they decided to start out early with a jazz piano bar. Laura was asked for her ID on the way in, which was an ego boost considering that she was now 32.

Jeff and his friend scooted up to the table in no time flat. He was there with people from his office. He was leaving in a few minutes to pick up his boss and they were all going out to eat. Jeff had all the requirements. White, Anglo-Saxon Protestant, Thirties, Divorced, Two small children, A college education, He appeared to be kind, and was reasonably nice looking. He was about six feet with blond hair and blue eyes. Fit and trim. Nice.

Everyone went to eat together. Laura and Jeff spent some time together afterwards. The next day he came over and went swimming. After the beach trip ended, they decided to see each other some more.

Jeff paid attention to Laura's family and friends. He bought her gifts, took her to dinner, to hear bands, and he helped in the yard. Jeff seemed genuinely concerned with her welfare, begging for forgiveness when Laura discovered that he was not divorced when they met. He was separated, but not legally divorced. He got divorced. Laura met his children and they all got along fine.

When he proposed, Laura thought that she had found the person that she would spend the rest of her life with. She would be set. She would have children and dreams come true. Anyone reading this that has ever been married to an alcoholic or drug addict will know how this turns out and could actually write the rest of this story.

Planning the wedding and having the wedding was great fun. Laura could do and wear exactly what she wanted. Though it was a small wedding, it had all the thrills. Laura wore an off-white suit with a lavender-knit dressy sweater sporting a collar decorated with pearls. She made her headdress. It was covered in pearls and had a short veil. She carried white roses and lavender orchids. Dianne was her only attendant. Donny, Jeff's best friend, was the best man.

After the reception at Louise's, Laura's Aunt, the lucky couple took off for a five-day honeymoon in New Orleans. It was magic. Once, during a storm, the lights went out in the hotel, Laura lit the candles she brought with her in her suitcase. They recorded the music playing on the radio so they could play the tapes later. They had their first argument and made up.

They moved into Laura's house. It was a long drive each day for Jeff to get to work, but he said that he didn't mind. Eventually, they might move, but for now everything was fine.

Laura got pregnant three weeks after she got married. She would deliver her first child at the age of thirty-five. So be it. Walker and Susan, Jeff's children, spent a lot of time with Laura. Once, when Jeff was out of town for a week, Laura kept them by herself. They played everyday. Hard. Emily, Jeff's ex-wife was moving from their house into a trailer and had no water. Jeff had filed bankruptcy three months before the wedding. This was a bad sign but Laura was sure that her good credit would see them through. She had no experience with bad credit or alcoholism.

Jeff drank everyday on the way home from work. By the time he hit the front door he had consumed a bottle of wine or a six-pack. In September, Laura took the calendar from her checkbook and circled the days that Jeff had not been drinking. To her surprise, the only days that Jeff did not drink were the days that one of his children was there for the weekend.

Jeff borrowed money from Laura's savings to get Emily set up in the trailer. He got more money to buy the furniture he wanted for the nursery.

Walker came to live with them. Jeff paid Emily $10,000 for him. Laura did not know about the money. She did not even know that it existed or that it was gone. She was six months pregnant.

Walker was thrilled to live with Laura and Jeff and he only had a small set of problems that he brought with him. Jeff felt that Emily was taking the divorce out on Walker and she was a little heavy with her hand. Walker was the only child Laura had ever seen that did not want to eat at McDonalds because Emily had fed her children there almost every night. It was going to take some adjusting because Walker was almost a nervous wreck. So the adjusting began.

David was born in February. He was the delight of Laura's life. Laura quit work two days before he arrived. She could devote her whole day to David and tried her best to do so. She could also give Walker the attention he needed when he got home from school.

Jeff was in the process of changing everything in the house. Laura figured that it was necessary for him to feel that it was his place. The drinking continued. Laura had hoped that Walker's arrival would make Jeff happier. She really knew nothing about alcoholics.

Money was pretty tight so in the fall Laura went back to work teaching half-days. It was the best of both worlds. She did not get tired of teaching and she did not get tired of being at home. She had her mornings free to play with David, visit her mom, clean house or grocery shop. It was great and it was going to last for the next four years.

Once, when David was six months old, Jeff was especially intoxicated. Laura picked David up out of his crib and made this promise, "No matter what happens, David, I promise that I will always be here for you and I will be sober."

It was also about this time that Jeff was drunk at the supper table. He was delivering his nightly monologue when Walker looked at him and said, "I hate you." Jeff flew into an absolute rage. He started screaming obscenities. He took his hands and slung everything off the table. Laura watched the baked beans stick to the wallpaper. She grabbed David and Walker to move them away from the flying glass. It was too late for Walker. He had already cut his toe. Jeff flew out the door and took off in his car.

Laura doctored Walker as best she could mentally and physically. He cried. He was scared. Laura picked up the phone and called the police to tell them that an enraged drunk was driving around town in a brown Cressida. She put the children to bed, cleaned up the mess, and went to bed herself. Jeff never apologized, much less, never even mentioned the event.

During that winter Laura developed a cough. She remembered that several years ago her doctor had given her a prescription for cough syrup with "Fill as needed" on the side. She was hoping that it was still good when she stopped by the pharmacy and asked for it. The man at the counter said, "Just a minute" and went to the back. In a minute the head pharmacist and storeowner came to the counter and said that he could not fill the prescription. Laura said, "Okay, I was just hoping that it would still be good. Do I need to call my doctor for a new prescription?" "No, there is another problem," replied the druggist; "Your husband has been in here every other day for a long time getting this cough syrup refilled. We really did not know what to do about it, but we can't fill it again until tomorrow." Laura was horrified. She was embarrassed. And finally she was mad as hell. She remembered one of the few things her mother had ever said about alcoholics, sometimes they drink vanilla flavoring and sometimes they drink cough syrup.

In the discussion that followed with Jeff that evening, Laura held back no emotions. She put all the cards on the table about his condition. Jeff had always said that his mother and brother were alcoholics. Jeff was embarrassed about the cough syrup and could not think of why he was doing that; it just made him feel better. He would not do it again. He did not want anyone to think that he was an alcoholic because he certainly was not.

Jeff was fired from his job late that fall, even though he had been with the company for eleven years. The story was that Jeff and his boss had gotten into a fistfight over something. Laura had never known anyone who had been fired and really did not know what to think. She remembered how upset her father had been once because he had to fire an engineer for drinking on the job. They came for Jeff's car. In less than three weeks he had another job with another company doing basically the same thing and had another new Cressida.

Laura was sitting at the kitchen table one Saturday afternoon when Jeff came in from working in the yard. He told Laura that the side of his face hurt and he was afraid that he might need the bridge replaced that was done while he was in the Marines. Laura said that he should go to the dentist right away. Because Jeff had more than one job last year he would have extra money coming in from taxes. He had paid excess in social security tax.

The dentist did not replace the bridge. He suspected nerve damage and set him up an appointment with the Carolina School of Dentistry. He gave Jeff some Percodan to ease the pain and Jeff's life changed forever.

Laura went with Jeff for mouth surgery. They severed some nerves in Jeff's mouth but it did not take care of the pain. Jeff continued to consult doctors and to take Percodan.

It was decided that Jeff should have neurosurgery at High Point Regional Hospital. The surgery was to sever some nerves in Jeff's neck to help relieve the pain. Laura went with him. After work each day she would gather David and Walker, drive to High Point, leave the children with Jeff's mother and go to the hospital. At the end of visiting hours she would pick up the kids and drive over an hour to get back home. Jeff seemed to be enjoying his hospital stay. He had lots of company and flirted heavily with the nurses.

Everything changed when the pain medicine stopped. When Jeff was not given the pain medicine he demanded, he pulled out his IV and left the hospital. It was a close call to get insurance to pay for his treatment.

The next recommended step for Jeff was to try a pain clinic. Laura took him to be evaluated because he was so stoned that he could not drive. In fact, he could hardly walk. Taking two minutes to go twenty feet, he was in slow motion. They stopped his evaluation test after two hours because he only answered five questions, admitting him the next day. All was well for a few days. They were decreasing his pain medicine and trying to make him focus on pain control. Once again, when his medicine stopped, he packed his bags, left, and came home for Laura to take care of him.

For a while Laura thought that things were getting better. Jeff was not drinking. He was, Laura really believed, trying to manage his pain medicine. He was seeing several different doctors and trying to find out what was causing his face to hurt. All Laura wanted was the marriage she had hoped for to work. She wanted the problems solved and for their life to be better. With strong hopes that Jeff would get better, she wanted her husband to be well and she wanted her second child...a boy.

If anyone knew the truth about what was happening in her marriage, they would think that she was crazy. Maybe so. She had told some people some of the events, but not everything to anybody. There were two children in her family and Dianne and she were very close. Laura wanted that for David. David was the light of her life. She had never known such love. She could only imagine the blessings that two sons would bring. She had read up on all the "wives' tales" of how to better the odds of having a boy.

Jeff did not mind. He was all for another child. The problem was having the sex. Jeff was not functioning well in that area. All those drugs were taking their toll. Laura had to come up with a subtle plan for making this work. From the timing of her pregnancy with David, she pretty much knew when she ovulated. So she had to check the calendar for a month when that might fall on a weekend. Then she had to plan to have some time for Jeff and her to be alone. She would have to control the whole day in order to be successful with the sex. Well, trying to control a whole day when the "controlee" was on drugs was totally impossible so this would have to be done in the morning.

When the morning came and all children were safely somewhere else, Laura went to work. She switched from homemaker, mother, and teacher to seductress. Lady Chatterley, Jezebel, and all the rest could have taken lessons. Jeff could only function to have sex every six months or so. He talked about it a lot and sometimes made some effort, but drugs are drugs. Laura took Jeff by the hand and led him into the bedroom. She knew that if this were successful she would be working the rest of her life and would have no time to herself. Not caring, she really wanted the child and she needed the sex. She could have "seduced a German", as her friend, Donna use to say. All was going very well and Jeff was really doing his part. Now, according to everything she had read, those little XX sperms were plentiful, but the XY's were much better swimmers. She knew that she had to be in the best position to insure a boy. She took the chance and it went okay. Laura enjoyed the sex; Jeff was in a state of shock. Three weeks later Laura missed her period.

Please don't think that Laura would not have loved a daughter. She would have. For the family situation, meaning Susan's being more jealous of a girl, and for David, a boy was what she wanted.

With a new outlook on life, Laura's life was looking up, the best of jobs and the best of mornings with David. Jeff was taking as much Percodan as he could get his hands on because his face still hurt. Walker was doing better but Susan came and went. This was the calm before the storm.

Jeff's doctor arranged for him to have some surgery at Duke. It was to be in August when Laura was out of school and seven months pregnant. Walker stayed with friends, David stayed with Grandmaw, and Laura went to Durham with Jeff. She figured she could just spend the night in Jeff's room once they took him to surgery. She had not counted on their taking the bed too. By the time Laura could see Jeff she was exhausted. Dollars were getting pretty tight at home, so she had figured out that if she went to the car about five AM, there was no attendant on duty. She could drive around the block, reenter the parking garage and get a new ticket, anything for a diversion and to save a buck. Back in the hospital Jeff was pleading for pain medicine. He begged Laura to talk to the doctor. When Laura finally found the doctor he said, "Your husband has all the pain medicine he can have. I will not give him anymore. He has more than one problem and if I see that he has upset you again, I will send you home. You need to take care of yourself. He will be just fine." That was not what she expected to hear, but it seemed pretty final. In another day her Mom and Dianne came to take her home. They would be back for Jeff in a week. Laura could not stand being away from David any longer.

Dylan was born in late September. Laura worked through Wednesday and Dylan was born on Friday. All that Laura could want was in her arms. A size smaller and a shade lighter than David, he was perfect, just like his brother.

Laura was a little concerned about home. She had planned everything for David's rides and sitters. However, Jeff changed everything then could not keep anything straight. He had it all arranged for all of the children to be at home when Dylan came. After a C-section she hoped she could handle it.

Things were moving very fast. Jeff's company relocated him two hours away so some nights he stayed out of town. Laura went back to work after eight weeks. David was in pre-school two mornings a week. Annie, the world's best sitter, picked him up and looked after both boys while Laura worked in the afternoon.

In November Jeff had more surgery. This time it was in Pittsburgh with a specialist in facial pain. Dylan was just over eight weeks and was breast-fed. David stayed with Grandmaw at Dianne's. Walker stayed with friends. Dianne and Laura and Dylan flew to Pittsburgh for Laura to be there during the surgery. The teachers at work gave Laura $200 to help with expenses. The surgery went well so Laura and crew left for home. They got back in town just in time to get David and Walker to the Christmas parade. It seemed like a year since Laura had slept. She opted for individual turkey breasts for Thanksgiving dinner and a glass of wine or two.

Jeff came home and they made it through Christmas, but went back to Pittsburgh for more surgery in February. Laura flew up with him to make sure he got to the hospital okay. He was very heavy into Percodan. When he was all settled in his room, he had a grand maul seizure. Laura had never seen anything like this. She went running out in the hall screaming for help. Jeff was shaking all over, his eyes rolled back in his head, and he was foaming at the mouth! The nurse said not to worry. She said that he was in withdrawal from all the drugs and he would be fine. She sent Laura back to the motel. Laura saw Jeff for a minute before the surgery and waited until he was awake and okay before she left for home.

There were still wonderful things in her life. David and Dylan were cute as buttons. One of David's back teeth turned a little dark and they went to the dentist. Several weeks later they were at Grandmaw's and David said, "There are four things I don't do."

Grandmaw said, "What are they?"

"I don't talk to strangers. I don't say bad words. I don't do drugs and I don't like the dentist." What a comment on the condition of society. Laura wrote it down and hung it on Grandmaw's refrigerator.

In April Jeff called Laura at work. He wanted her to call his doctor and ask him to give him some Percodan for pain. Jeff was getting Percodan from several doctors and Laura could not imagine how he could be without. But, she called the doctor. He came to the phone to talk to her. He told her that he would never give Jeff another prescription. He said, "Do you not know what he did?"

"No."

"Well, he took the last prescription I wrote and he changed it to prescribe more Percodan. He was arrested. You need to ask him about it."

Laura thanked the doctor for talking to her. She was standing in the middle of the teacher's lounge. It was the same feeling but on a much larger scale that had run through her body when she heard about the cough syrup.

When Jeff called back he was furious at the doctor. He had the whole thing handled. He had an attorney and the judge said that if nothing else happened in five years the whole thing would be expunged.

Laura was getting scared with so much happening. Jeff's company found out about the drugs and let him go so he had to turn in another car. Walker made an "F" in Algebra. Jeff said that he would handle it. He handled it by taking fourteen Valium and going to bed.

Once Jeff called Laura from the grocery store to see if the boys were suppose to be with him. If they were, he had lost them. They were at home, but Jeff was beginning to have blackouts. One day he had another seizure in the kitchen and dropped Dylan on the floor. He took Laura's dog, Bo Jangles, of eleven years to the vet. Bo Jangles had some bad spots and an infection. Telling the vet to cure him or put him out of his misery, Jeff signed papers but was too stoned to know what he was doing. When he went to pick up the dog, the doctor had put him to sleep. Jeff carried on so badly that it was a week before Laura could allow herself to grieve.

It's not that Jeff wasn't being cared for. He went to three or four doctors. The major problem was that he would not accept any treatment unless it involved narcotics or surgery. He would not give anything else a try. He took more Percodan than any one doctor would prescribe. When he ran completely out of drugs the whole family would sit for hours in an emergency room waiting for Jeff to get a shot of Demerol. He blamed all of this on his tolerance build up, something that his doctors could not understand. His face did not hurt all the time, but when it did, it was brutal. One doctor explained to Laura that the drugs were not helping this type of pain because they actually made the pain seem worse and the addiction was terrible.

One very cold weekend, even during an ice storm, all of the children were together at the house. Walker came up to Laura and said, "Has Dad gone to kill himself?"

"Heavens, no! He's in the bathroom"

"No he's not. He just left the water running so you would think that he is in there."

Laura checked and Walker was right. Jeff had always said that suicide was perfectly fine, talked about it a lot, and even had books on it. Laura called the police. She got all the children on the bed. They held hands and prayed that Jeff would be okay. Then they continued to do whatever they could do. In a couple of hours the phone rang. The Rescue Squad had picked Jeff up and he was in the hospital. It seems that he had parked his car and was out walking in a field with the freezing rain coming down. He had hopes of freezing to death. When Laura got to the hospital, he begged her to get the doctor to give him some Percodan. The doctor gave him nine. Instantly fine with this, Laura took Jeff home.

Laura treated her husband with all the love and respect that she could muster. It was hard to keep so much focus on him when she had a job, two small children, a teenager, a house to run, and bills to pay.

Jeff got another job back in the same city as his old job. He had an hour drive, but at least it wasn't two hours. He got a car allowance and chose a Supra. It was just a small irritation to Laura. When they had gotten married Laura had a 240Z. When David was born, Jeff made her sell it because he said that it was too small for the family. She drove a Gremlin for six months until they could manage a van. Regardless of the resentment, Laura was very thankful that Jeff had another job.

They took off for the beach for a few days. Jeff wanted to stop at a mall on the way, saying he needed to pick up some things, but he would be right out. Everyone waited in the car for Jeff. After an hour and a half, Laura left the children to go find him. When he saw her he was very surprised. He said that he had forgotten they were with him.

Jeff went back to Pittsburgh for one more surgery. Trying to hold her family together, Laura stayed with Walker and her children.

Jeff went back to work too soon after this surgery, but still taking too much medication. He came home again to say that he had been fired.

Laura called to talk to his boss. Though he was very nice, his boss said that Jeff had used up all his sick days and then some. They really needed for him to get well, but they could not allow him to do that at work. Laura asked about disability since he had insurance to cover that. His boss gave Laura the number to call and said he thought that would be a good idea. Later that night Laura got a phone call from one of Jeff's friends at work. He told Laura that Jeff needed some professional help, that he had a major drug problem. He said that they had tried to talk with him and work with him, but Jeff would not listen. Defiantly, Jeff moved his desk and office stuff out to the parking lot and was going to work out there. When the boss saw him he was fired.

Jeff felt betrayed by his friends. Laura was numb. Again.

It takes awhile for disability. It takes six months for Social Security disability. Despite Laura's returning to work full-time, there was very little money. Laura's Mom bought David's clothes for school.

Jeff no longer had an allowance for the Supra. When the rear end began making noise, he took it to the dealer to be told that it would be

$1400 to fix it. Before it was all over, Jeff charged $3800 on Laura's credit card and came home with a new Cressida. Laura tried to explain to him that there was no way they could handle the car payments and credit card payments. Jeff just could not understand. They gave the car back and lost about $3000 in the process. That was better than spending an additional $12,000.

They were able to find a Triumph for Jeff and he was content for a few months.

He was still all about changing everything in the house as fast as possible.

One day he was coming down the highway and had car trouble. He had the car towed to a repair shop and called Laura to pick him up. They went back in three days to pick up the repaired car. When Laura asked what went wrong she was told that the car had been out of gas. Jeff was so stoned that he did not know that he was out of gas.

After picking up Susan one weekend, they stopped at a truck stop for gas. Jeff went in to pay. They waited and waited. Walker, Susan, and David went in to check on him. Laura waited and waited. Finally, she got Dylan out of his car seat and went in herself. She could not believe her eyes. There stood Jeff at the counter with all the children and about ten very irritated truck drivers behind him. Jeff had all the contents of his wallet spread all over the counter along with everything out of his pockets. He had separated the bill into three different sections and was trying to figure out how to sign his name. The lady behind the counter looked at Laura and said, "Are you with him?"

"Yes."

"Can you do something to help? I don't want to call the police."

Laura grabbed up Jeff's things, signed the card and headed out at top speed. It was a quiet ride home.

Life totally fell apart the day Jeff was late coming back from picking up Walker from his Mother's. Jeff was completely out of it when he came in the door. Laura said, "How was it possible for you to drive in your condition?"

"I didn't drive." Jeff replied as he fell against the door, "Walker drove."

"You had a fourteen year old drive down the interstate because you were too stoned?"

"Yes. We got home fine. It's okay."

"It is not okay. I have had it. You must decide between your family and Percodan and you must decide right now."

"Are you saying that I have to quit taking Percodan or I have to leave?"

"Yes."

"Now?"

"Yes, right now."

Jeff turned to Walker and said, "Pack your bags, son. We are leaving."

Walker looked at his Dad and said, "No. I'm not going. I'm staying here with Laura."

Laura could not believe what she had heard. She could not believe that Jeff thought he would take Walker and she could not believe that Walker had told him he wasn't going. Jeff flew into a rage, packed some bags, and left. Laura was glad that he was gone. She sat on the sofa holding Dylan and trying to answer David's questions. Walker was not upset at all. Relief filled the room.

No one heard from Jeff for a few days. Laura did not try to find him. She took her children to the county fair, but upon returning, Jeff was there. He said that he would never take Percodan again. He would try Darvocet.

Jeff pretty much remained stoned on the sofa. Annie came in the mornings and took care of David and Dylan. She was wonderful and it was nice to have an adult in the house that Laura could talk to.

Pretty soon the nurse from the insurance disability office began making calls. When she finally came around to see Jeff he told her that his pain was so bad that he had just taken eight Darvocets. Shocked, the nurse didn't know the half of it. She did not know about all the Percodan, Valium, and Demerol shots.

The insurance company decided that Jeff would have to go into a drug rehab before they would okay disability. He would be gone for six weeks. Laura was required to attend Alanon meetings.

Her very good friend, Di, went with her to her first meeting. Realizing that she was not alone, Laura felt so much better. She also realized that she was not invisible. She had been feeling like she was completely gray and there was nothing to her anymore. She had been trying to read and could not finish more than a paragraph before her thoughts would turn to Jeff and the disaster she was living. Alanon began to allow her to focus on something besides Jeff. She would be okay and could enjoy her children even more. Even though she had to drive three hours twice a week to see Jeff, her life was better. The tranquility in her home was wonderful.

Jeff was having fits, calling every day to say that he did not belong in rehab. He made her promise every day that she would talk to the doctors to try to get him out but because he behaved so badly they kept him an extra two weeks.

Jeff came out of rehab mad at the world, especially Laura. The way he looked at her was so scary that it gave her chills. She knew that he wanted to kill her but she was trying to focus on something besides him. He did not go back to prescription drugs. He did develop a fondness for champagne, drinking at least two bottles a day. One evening on his return from buying more champagne he began backing up the driveway extremely fast. Laura dragged Dylan out of the way just in time to keep Jeff from running over his legs.

Finally, all of the doctors and insurance people got together, so the checks began to arrive. It was wonderful to have a little money coming in. There would never be as much as there was before but two-thirds of it was much better than nothing. Laura's full time salary was helping, too. She had excellent insurance coverage for the family. Jeff was put on Methadone. This drug would take care of the pain and the addiction and he would not be high. Never mind that it was more addictive than heroin and would change his personality.

Methadone actually improved their life style, but Laura still went to meetings. There were many times when Jeff would run out of the drug. He never took the prescription as prescribed; always took too much at the beginning. He would have what the doctor called "break through pain" and the whole family would have to head for the emergency room for his shot. Then there were the times when he would still drink.

When the Social Security money came in everyone was on cloud nine. Finally, some bills could be paid and there would be some room to breath. The money was retroactive which means they got the past six months worth all at one time. Laura figured that the system was set up that way to keep out people who were not really disabled. If you could go that long without money, you had to be disabled. Otherwise you would have found a job to keep from starving.

Jeff came home one day with a Corvette. It was not new, but it was still expensive. When he was asked how he paid for it, he said, "Well, I sold the Triumph and I had managed to stash a little money away." Laura had some real trouble understanding this. The next day the engine blew and it took the rest of the Social Security money to fix it.

In December a check started coming for the children. Laura felt like they might make it after all.

In January Laura opened the information sent from Social Security to be used for taxes. There was this huge amount listed for the children, but Laura had only received one check. She went to Jeff with this crazy paper thinking he would be concerned. He looked at her and said, "Oh, that money came. That's the money I used to buy the Vet." Son of a Bitch! Laura began to hate the Corvette. She had never really liked them very much to begin with, and she never really cared that much for the Beach Boys either. She had just about preferred Peter, Paul, and Mary over the Beatles. And she wasn't too sure of her feelings for Jeff now, either.

One afternoon Laura went back to the bedroom and found Jeff in the bed. He said, "I can't go on like this. I can't go on." He kept repeating it over and over. Laura did not know if he was serious or if he was pulling her chain to get some drugs. But she had received some help for herself. She called the mental health clinic. After signing papers at the Sheriff's Department, she took Walker, David, and Dylan to Di's house and waited. The deputies came to the house and took Jeff to the hospital in chains. They put him on suicide watch for four days and then sent him home. It would be seven more years before any more suicide attempts occurred. When Jeff finally asked Laura why she had him committed, she replied, "If you had killed yourself, and your children ever asked me if I had done anything to stop it, I wanted to be able to say, 'Yes'."

It was also about this time that Dianne had a house fire. No one was hurt but the house was a mess from the fire and water damage. Charles decided that it was time to move the family to Wilmington where he would start a new business. He figured that as long as the insurance company was paying for a place until the house was fixed, it might as well be in Wilmington. Grandmaw and Laura were pretty upset. Laura had to ask her friend, Di, to be her substitute sister while Dianne was gone.

Laura's family was entering another dimension. Spending money became Jeff's third disease. He was taking out credit cards in Laura's name. He would fill out the application using her social security number and he would use initials for the name so he could sign them without question. The mail came when Laura was at work so he could take the credit card and use it without her knowledge until the bill came in. Laura would open up a bill she did not know was coming and see a balance for $3500. She would have a fit. Some of it was cash that Jeff was giving to relatives. Much of it was for tools he was using in the garage. None of it was ever returnable. Laura had to pay the bill or have her husband arrested for forgery and still pay the bill.

She tried and tried to talk to Jeff. Jeff bought everything. He told Annie to hide the mail if he was not home when it came and not to give Laura's mail to her. Annie did this for a while, but she could not continue. She finally told Laura.

Sex. Does anyone remember about the sex? Once, when Dylan was two, Jeff attempted to have sex with Laura. It did not work. Methadone was no better for sex than Percodan. It was their last attempt. Ever. Nevermore.

Pretty soon Jeff got himself scheduled for more surgery at Duke. This time Laura checked into a motel in Durham right across from the hospital. Laura's Mom was showing some signs of Alzheimer's disease so she was afraid to leave the boys with her. Di spent the weekend at her house to watch them. Then, on Sunday, because she was coming to Durham to visit family, she brought Laura's Mom, David, and Dylan to the hospital. She could only see Jeff for a few minutes every four hours so she felt safe with her Mom watching the young ones during that short time. David was a big help with Dylan. Once Jeff was in a regular room Laura headed for home. It would be a couple of weeks before she would come back for him. He was already arguing with the doctor about medication.

The weekend that Jeff was to come home, Walker spent with his Mother. Laura picked up Jeff on Sunday and then drove to pick up Walker. Walker told Laura that he had something that he needed to tell his Dad and it was really serious. Laura said that since his Dad had just had major surgery, Walker should run it past her first. Now, at this time Walker was almost seventeen and a rising senior, Susan was twelve and a rising seventh grader, David was seven and Dylan was three.

This was the story. Emily was physically abusing Susan. Everyone had known for some time that Emily would slap Susan. Walker and Jeff had both witnessed it. Susan did not always know when it was coming, and she had learned two lessons very well, one to lie, and the other to duck.

Anyway, Walker, Susan, and Emily were eating dinner and Susan spilled a glass of tea. Emily told her to clean it up. When Susan returned with the towel, Emily slapped Susan down to the floor, jumped on top of her and began choking her to the point Susan could not breathe. Walker had to pull Emily away from Susan. Laura was very upset and felt a little like she was living on Tobacco Road. She knew that this could not be allowed to continue, and she hoped that God would give her the strength she needed.

Laura had not lost her religion. In fact, it was her survival. She had been teaching Sunday school at the Presbyterian Church until they started attending the Methodist Church down the street. It was Annie's church. Walker was really happy because he had a better view of the choir. David was not so happy because all of his Pre-School friends were at the Presbyterian Church. Laura was fine because this was a "working man's" church and the clothes did not have to be so fancy and expensive. Everyone liked that. Jeff did not like anything or anyone and did his best to hold them up or keep them from going every single Sunday.

Laura wanted to be able to present Jeff with a solution, not just a problem. She called Susan. She told Susan what Walker had said and asked if that was what happened. Susan said that it was. She asked if there was anything more she wanted to add or anything she wanted to take away. Susan said that there was not. Laura reminded Susan that school would be out in a week. She wanted to know if Susan thought she would be safe for that long. Susan said, "Yes." Laura asked Susan if she would like to come and live with them. Again, "Yes." Laura told her that she needed to do some things. One, Susan needed to take one of her school notebooks and for the next week or until they came for her, she should write down every time her mother hit her. If she knew why, she should write that down also and date it. Next, she wanted Susan to start gathering her favorite things. She should just put them, little by little, in a corner of her room or somewhere out of the way. If her mom asked what she was doing, just say that she might take them when she went to visit her dad for the summer. Susan had always spent most of every summer with Laura and Jeff. And last, Susan needed to talk to the guidance counselor at school (her dad would also call) just in case there was some emergency and Susan needed help fast. Susan agreed. Laura presented the whole thing to Jeff and they made plans for Susan to move in.

The house only had three bedrooms. Walker had his own while David and Dylan shared. Walker was keeping his own room because he was to be a senior and he deserved it. For the next year Susan would sleep on the top bunk in David's room and Dylan would sleep with Jeff and Laura. Then when Walker went into the Marines (as planned), Susan would have her own room, and David and Dylan would share the largest room.

Jeff seemed to do better with Susan there. Laura just let Susan play. She was hoping they would all bond and become a family.

Two months later Emily called because she had not received child support for the month of July. Jeff told her that he was not going to send her child support because Susan was and would continue to live with him. Emily flipped out, as most any mother would. She said that was not going to happen and she was coming to pick up Susan. Jeff went over with her why it was going to happen, but she would not listen. She said she was on her way and asked for directions to get to the house. Jeff gave her the directions and got off the phone. He called Social Services and asked what he should do. He was told, "Don't be at home and start custody proceedings immediately". So the whole family packed up to leave for however long it would take. Once they were well away, Laura began processing the whole thing. The one thought that made her crazy was that Walker had been living in that house for almost nine years and his mother didn't know where it was. That spoke volumes.

In no time at all, Jeff and Emily met with an attorney and Jeff became the custodial parent. This time it did not cost $10,000.

They ran completely out of money. Jeff was spending $12,000 more a year than they were bringing in. Laura could not pay the minimum amounts on the credit cards. They went to the bank and took out a $45,000 second mortgage against the house. Jeff had thirty-two credit cards in her name. Laura hoped that this experience would stop Jeff's spending. Wrong Again!

Susan was not bonding well. She was having some trouble with not always being the princess. There is a myth about bringing a child into your home that has been the victim of bad parenting. Laura read this one day sitting in a doctor's office waiting for Jeff. The myth is that a child who is brought into a home that offers security, warmth, well-being, and love will grow, bond and love the new family. The truth is that the child will resent the non-parent for being a better parent than the one they left. This was beginning to show with Susan. She was saying really bad things about Laura behind her back at school. One day the assistant principal came to Laura's room to tell her that Susan had been kicked off the school bus for calling someone a bitch. Now, it would be up to Laura to have Susan everyday in her room until it was time to go home.

Hurricane Hugo came and went. There were nine trees down in the yard. There was no electricity for five days. Jeff rounded up Grandmaw and some propane for the lanterns and grill and Laura became a grill master. She could fix coffee, biscuits, and even French fries. Ice did not exist so she cooked the meat as it thawed out in the freezer. Stores could only sell items if you had the exact change. Everyone went to bed early and got up early. The schools reopened twelve hours after the lights came back on. Laura had never seen such dirt. And bees, why were there so many bees?

The river cabin suffered a lot of damage. Grandmaw had canceled the insurance on it because she thought it was too expensive. Jeff volunteered to fix it. Dianne and Charles would help pay for it. Jeff spent days at the river. What a good break for the family. He could take his drugs like he wanted and his family could experience more tranquility.

Things were still going well with Walker, David and Dylan. Laura was very glad for that. Thanksgiving was coming up and although Laura was not feeling very well, she was planning a big family dinner. If it wasn't for some very strong over-the-counter medicine, she wasn't sure she would make it. Her mother was to be there for the meal, then go home to be with Dianne and her family when they finished their meal at Charles's mother's house. It was getting more and more difficult for Laura's Mom. Everyone felt sure that she had Alzheimer's but no one knew exactly what to do about it. Her personality was changing. She said some pretty mean things. So the scene was set for a disaster.

Jeff and David finished up early and when Dylan got sleepy, the three of them took off to the bedroom. That left Walker, Laura, Susan, and Grandmaw at the table. Susan got up to get seconds and came back to the table with her plate piled high, real high. Now, Susan had always carried a little extra weight, but she was not what anyone would call fat. Laura figured that when she hit her growth spurt that she would end up just fine. Laura's Mom took one look at Susan and her plate and said, "Well, it's no wonder that you are so fat. Just look at all that food on your plate."

Walker, who had been leaning back in his chair, sat up straight with his mouth hanging open. Susan sat down her plate sobbing, left the table and headed for the bedroom. Laura was thinking about as fast as she could think. She said, "Mom, that wasn't very nice. You really hurt Susan's feelings." Her Mom said, "Well, she is fat and she needs to watch what she eats." Laura could see that Walker was beginning to regain his composure and she said to him, "Walker, please sit here for a minute with Grandmaw, I'm going to check on Dylan."

When Laura entered her bedroom Jeff, Susan, David, and Dylan were all on the bed. Laura listened for a minute, but she couldn't stay long, because Walker would only be able to do so much. She tried to explain that her Mother was sick and then went to the phone. She called Dianne and said, "I want you to wait 5 minutes and call Mother. Tell her that y'all are about to leave and that she needs to head home for the dessert party."

Dianne said, "We are not that close."

Laura said, "It doesn't matter," and told her what had happened. Dianne agreed.

Laura went back to the table and sat down. She started finishing her meal, telling Walker that his Dad needed him to help with Dylan so he could escape. Laura visited with her Mom as if nothing had happened. In a few minutes the phone rang and it was Dianne for Grandmaw.

Grandmaw protested some. She probably suspected, but she let Laura pack her up some leftovers and they had a nice drive back to Charlotte. Grandmaw seemed to have forgotten the whole thing by the time she got to her house. Laura really felt that it would not be too long before Dianne arrived. On the way home Laura started feeling really bad. Her medicine had run out, she had a forty-minute drive, she was dead tired, and she knew she had hurt feelings and a very messy kitchen to face when she got home.

Life has its good moments. Sometimes they are far enough in between that you forget they exist. Laura had one when she walked in the door. There was no mess! There was not a dirty dish. There was not a dirty piece of china or silver. All the food was put away. Walker was standing in the kitchen. Laura said, "Did you do this?"

Walker replied, "Yes, I thought you could use a hand." Laura could not thank him enough. She took some medicine and went to bed. She knew in her heart that no matter what Walker might do for the rest of his life; Laura would never ask anything else of him. She would just love him.

Laura went to the doctor the next day to discover that she had pneumonia. Dylan came down with it on Monday and was put in the hospital for the week that Laura was too sick to go to school, so she spent the days with Dylan in the hospital. She would get up, make sure everyone got to school and go to the hospital. She would stay until Jeff came to relieve her around six. She would go home, take care of dinner and homework and get ready for the next day shift. Dylan looked so small and helpless in that big bed. He had a wooden splint on his arm to hold in his

IV. Laura played games with him, read to him and thanked the Lord for making him better. He stayed five days and then they both went home to rest some more.

Jeff was still experiencing "break-through pain". Only now there was another issue. He was getting prescriptions for Demerol to help handle the pain so that his family did not have to spend every other day in the emergency room. Unfortunately, the Demerol lowered his threshold for seizures. He had one under the Christmas tree and terrified the children. Laura was at work so they ran next door for help. Anyone else would have lost his drivers license, but not Jeff.

Still, life settled in for the holidays. Laura cooked most every meal. She made the Christmas presents. Jeff sold the Corvette and bought an old truck. Walker was finishing high school and getting ready for the Marines. The whole family watched the Desert Storm War on TV.

Walker had a date for the prom! Everyone was excited and making plans. A tux was rented along with a fine car. Laura had never seen Walker look so handsome. He asked her to help with the studs on his shirt and his cuff links. As Laura fixed his shirt she thought about how lucky she was. For a fleeting moment she almost felt sorry for Emily. After all, this should have been her moment, but she had messed it up so badly. Laura continued to enjoy her pleasure.

Walker graduated and went into the Marines. Laura really missed him. She could not imagine how things would change in the next four years. She thought that maybe the finances would improve. They did not. It had not even been a year since the whopping second mortgage. They were now another $18,000 in debt. Jeff had purchased every tool known to man. He still spent money like he was a chief executive. Laura would wake up in the middle of the night in cold sweats about the finances. When she woke up in the mornings she had the thirty seconds of peace before reality hit her. In September she told Jeff that they were not going to make it and they would be filing bankruptcy.

Laura made sure that the bankruptcy would be set up so they would pay everything they owed, but at lower interest. It was a most humiliating experience. Laura felt like such a failure. One lady even gave her advice on how to pack a healthy, but inexpensive, lunch for the kids. Laura had been doing this for years and better than this lady could advise, but she sat still and listened. She could only hope that Jeff was doing the same.

Laura was thrilled that someone had finally been able to get Jeff under control. She did not mind cutting even more corners to have the spending stopped. They were obligated to pay $800 dollars a month for the next six years. This included the second mortgage and car payments.

Jeff was still having seizures. Susan was still having adjustment problems, but Walker was doing well in the Marines. Grandmaw's mind was still getting worse, so Laura was going to Charlotte three times a week to take her out to eat and see to it that she had food in sight that did not have to be cooked. Her car had been removed from the garage and she accepted the fact that it was somewhere being fixed. David and Dylan were becoming Laura's sole source of joy.

One day Aunt Cathy called to say that she had been talking with Laura's Mom and that her Mom was planning on walking to the store. This meant that she would be wandering down a very busy street and would probably be lost forever. Aunt Cathy had called a neighbor to take her to the store and called Laura to let her know what was going on. That was the end of an era and Grandmaw could no longer be trusted alone. Jeff took Laura's Mom to stay with Dianne the next day. Charles came by a few days later and picked up clothes. Grandmaw would be safe with Dianne and Laura would start the search for a nursing home.

That summer Susan started hearing voices. (What?! Yeah, that's what I'm talking about.) Jeff took her for help and was told that she was "borderline" schizophrenic. Susan was placed in a mental institution for two weeks. It cost a fortune. When she came out she had some pills to take, was even more distant from her family, and had formed a new set of friends. It was a long, slow process getting her unattached. Laura was very concerned about Susan. Her attitude was bringing hardships on herself and her family. Laura was worried about her influence on David and Dylan. Susan was very careful to show David satanic symbols and scare him. She wanted to be a witch. There were no consequences for anything Susan did wrong. Jeff said that she had been punished enough by Emily. It was a big mess that Laura was sure would be getting bigger. Susan seemed to do everything she could to go against the grain.

Laura got an opportunity for a different job with the same system. She would be working twelve months rather than ten, which would give her a 20% raise. She would miss her children in the summer, but David was ten and she knew he would call if Susan or Dad or Dylan had a problem. The extra money helped Laura to breathe a little. She increased her payment for the bankruptcy hoping to end it earlier.

Life continued down the same path. Dianne was getting more and more stressed with looking after Grandmaw. Jeff continued to take his medicine all at once, have breakthrough pain, withdrawals, and seizures. The family still spent hours in waiting rooms for him to get shots. When they went to church, Jeff would make paper airplanes out of the bulletins or he would go to sleep and snore. It made Laura furious. He was worse than the kids. Susan continued to cause conflict. The first year she had her driver's license she had fourteen wrecks, eight of them in the driveway. The first one was at the highway patrol station when she went for her license. She locked bumpers with a car in the parking lot. She totaled the car that belonged to Laura's mother. David continued to worry about his Dad when he was at school. Sometimes his anxiety was terrible, so Laura began taking him to a doctor. The only outlet afforded to Laura was the Jimmy Buffett concert. Dianne still made sure that the two of them went each year. It was Laura's only chance to sing and dance and celebrate and laugh out loud. Other people were beginning to catch on to how much fun they had and were asking to go with them. One of them was Di, Laura's friend.

The secretary at Laura's new job asked her how she could live like this. She said it was crazy for Laura to go to Alanon. It was Jeff that needed to change, not her. Then she asked if Laura still loved Jeff. Laura replied, "Sometimes it's pretty tough, but I've been through one divorce and I don't want to go through another one. I don't even think I could afford it. Jeff does work with the boys and shows them how to do things. Anyway, when the bad outweighs the good, I'll do something. Right now, I'm still hoping that things will get better."

When David entered the sixth grade, he could no longer walk home from school with Dylan. Jeff's only responsibility was to pick Dylan up after school. The poor child would wait everyday for twenty minutes and then a teacher would take him inside to call. Sometimes Jeff would be asleep and sometimes he couldn't be found. Laura would leave work to rescue her precious son.

On Palm Sunday of that year, Susan walked slowly into the den. The family had been to church and out to eat. Everyone, including Susan was still in church clothes. Susan announced, "I don't feel very good. I took 46 sleeping pills." Then she collapsed to the floor. Jeff picked her up and took her to the bathroom. Laura called 911. Jeff was trying to get Susan to throw up. Laura mixed up some salt water for Susan to drink. She threw up some and passed out again. Laura went to the street to signal for the fire trucks and ambulance. Susan was slipping away pretty fast. Jeff followed the ambulance to the hospital. Laura followed when Annie arrived to care for David and Dylan.

At the hospital the doctors were pretty concerned. It seemed that Susan was having a psychotic experience. They were not sure that she would come out of it. They were not sure as to what all she had taken. Laura ran into a preacher she knew and they prayed long and hard for Susan.

Susan pulled through and was admitted to another mental hospital. It was a week later that the family could visit. So after church on Easter the family traveled to see Susan. Susan's Mom never showed.

During the counseling and therapy that followed one doctor stated that there were two families living in their house. Jeff and Susan were one family. Laura and the boys were another. The doctors told Jeff that he needed to stop taking Methadone or be more responsible with his medicine. They told Laura that they could not understand how she was still with him. In fact, Laura was hearing this from several doctors at this point and from more than one friend.

The Buffett concert came. Di went with Laura and Dianne. At the concert Di met this fine fellow who was next to them on the lawn. She married him a year later to the day. Laura was the maid of honor and David and Dylan lit the candles. There was just a slight hint of a Buffett song as the couple headed back down the aisle. This was one of the only glimmers of hope during this time.

The next two years just blurred together. Laura saw Susan off and got the boys to school each day. Because Jeff had taken to sleeping in the living room they would exit out the back door so as not to disturb him. Jeff began abusing the pets. He let some of them go and beat on some of the others. Laura figured that it would be her turn pretty soon. Jeff would give her looks that would send chills down her spine. After work Laura would fix supper. Jeff would not eat with them. He would stay in the garage until everyone was finished then he would eat. Laura would see to homework, clothes, and then go back to the kitchen to clean it up. By this time, Jeff would be asleep on the sofa. They still had to spend hours in waiting rooms for Jeff to get shots and talk to doctors.

Susan was finding some jobs that removed her from the household somewhat. Laura was very careful to plan any social event during Jeff's "normal periods". If something fell during the other two weeks, it just couldn't be done.

They were on a crazy cycle. Jeff would get his prescription for Methadone and he would take way too much of it. So for a week, he was mega hyper and bouncing off the walls. You could not keep up with him if you tried. Then he would realize that he was going to run out of pills and take them fairly correctly for two weeks. That was the normal time. Then Jeff would be out of drugs. He would sit in the living room with all the lights off and blinds drawn for a week in withdrawals. Children could not be in the room. It was during this time that the family had to sit in waiting rooms at the hospital. Jeff would get between 200 and 300 milligrams of Demerol in his shots.

Once Jeff told Laura that he and David were going to go at it one day and she should not interfere. He also suspected that Laura was having an affair with one of David's teachers. This was really hard to understand because this guy was about fifteen years younger than Laura. She had worked with him before and it was easy to talk to him about David's grades. He was also David's coach and they did see each other on team days. But an affair was out of the question. Laura did miss all the things a good marriage brought, but she was not in the affair business. Jeff kept insisting that she would leave him and Laura said no, but sometimes wondered when. She prayed to God to take care of her family. Sometimes she would sit in the dark in her bathroom and try to be calm. Sometimes she just walked.

When Di's first anniversary rolled around she reminded Laura that the top of the wedding cake was stored in Laura's freezer and that she would need it soon.

Laura went to the garage where the freezer was located and to her surprise found it unplugged. She looked at Jeff, "Why is this unplugged?"

"I have been using the outlet."

"How long has it been unplugged?"

"About four days."

This was not the first time. Jeff had unplugged it a year ago and had ruined $100 worth of quiche and supplies for Di's reception. After all, it was Di's freezer that she was letting Laura use so Di should be able to count on her things staying frozen. Laura replaced everything then and created enough stink that she thought Jeff would remember. I guess not. Now Laura had to deal with a ruined cake and ruined food.

Laura called to see if anyone had a picture of the cake. She called the person who made the cake to see if they remembered it or could do another one. She had no luck. She called other people to see if they could bake a cake. No one could help on such short notice. She was frantic. She took a walk to clear her head and come up with a plan. Her knees were shaking. That was a sure sign of how upset she was.

She sent Jeff to the store to buy cakes with bunches of white icing. While he was gone she rounded up the cake decorating tools that Susan had used in a high school course.

When Jeff returned she scraped the icing off the cakes. She practiced with the colored icing until she could do some good decorating. It took a while. She was glad that this cake had not had flowers. It just had trim that was easy to copy. She would have to go to the craft store to buy the flowers for the top because Jeff had seen fit to throw them away. It was confession time for him. He had actually unplugged the freezer before and the cake had become all green and molded so he had thrown it out.

Finally, Laura was ready to ice the cake. She worked very carefully. The two layers looked really good to her, but she was not sure that they would fool Di. She put the cake in the refrigerator and called the family together for a conference. She had to wait a minute because the boys were playing with the pet ferrets in the living room. "I have put the cake in the refrigerator and I'm going to leave for a few minutes to get the flowers for the top. Please be very careful when you open the door because I have to take the cake to Di tomorrow afternoon and I can't let anything else happen to it."

Everyone replied, "Yes, Ma'am, we'll be careful."

As Laura was backing out of the driveway she looked up to see David and his friend coming out of the house carrying soft drinks. She knew that they probably came from the refrigerator and she hoped that all was well.

Laura found little roses just like the ones that had been on the original cake. She was so excited to get home and finish up this cake. She needed to freeze it overnight to make it look more real to Di. When she opened the refrigerator door she let out a gasp. What she saw was a pineapple juice can on top of the cake. The cake was a mess and it took her a second to recognize the little footprints covering it. David came up to her to see what was wrong. At that moment she looked to the door and saw a ferret resting on one of the shelves. He looked so cute sitting there with his little paws covered in white icing. Laura grabbed the ferret and handed it to David. "Take this thing before I have to kill it" was what she said.

Laura knew that she would have to begin again. She sent Jeff to another store for cakes. At least this time she knew that it could be done. David swore that he thought both the ferrets were running around the house playing. He had no idea that one of them had slipped into the refrigerator when they got out the drinks. That same ferret had done this once before, but there were no wedding cakes to mess up at that time.

Laura finished the cake and froze it overnight. The next day she packed it up and took it to Di's. Di pulled it out of the box and looked at it for a long, long time. Finally, she said slowly, "This isn't my cake, is it?"

Laura told her the story. Di was impressed that Laura had worked so hard to make things right. She said to Laura, "If you ever write your book, you must include this story."

Jeff's doctor got into a little trouble with prescriptions. She told Jeff that she was referring him to a specialist and she would give him no more methadone. He stopped sending her flowers. The new doctor did seem stricter with the medicine, but at this time it just made matters worse at home. There was still no clear diagnosis for Jeff. One doctor now thought that it was MS.

Laura continued to go to Alanon as often as she could and she began seeing a doctor at the mental health clinic. Most days she could do this at lunch so her job did not suffer. Her doctor told her that she was living under the sword of Damocles. She could live with that tension, but what was she going to do when it fell? And sooner or later it was going to fall.

# The Sword Falls

Now, Damocles was a member of the court of Dionysus II who ruled Syracuse, Sicily more that 300 years before Christ. Unfortunately, he talked too much about the opulence of his ruler. To teach Damocles a lesson, Dionysus invited him to a feast. Damocles found a sword suspended by a single hair, dangling over his head. It represented the constant danger that went with the wealth and happiness of Dionysus. Now, the "sword of Damocles" has become symbolic for the threat of danger.

It was the week before Easter. Laura was hard at work with several of her colleagues on a presentation for the next day's big meeting with the high-school principals when her phone rang. It was Jeff. The conversation went something like this; "I just called to tell you that everything will be alright. I know that you are a good mother and you will take good care of the boys."

"What are you talking about?"

"Well, I know that you can handle this. I want you to know that I love you."

"Handle what? What are you going to do?" Alarms were going off in Laura's head.

"I just wanted to say 'Goodbye'." And Jeff hung up.

With no hesitation at all, Laura pushed another line button and dialed 911. When the operator answered she repeated the conversation and said that her husband had a gun, felt sure that he had made the call from home and also felt sure that he was going to kill himself. She told the operator that she was heading home driving a burgundy minivan and it would take her about ten minutes to get there. She headed back to the lab where she informed her coworkers and two of them decided that they would be following her shortly.

On the way home she put on her flashers. About halfway there a policeman pulled her over. She said, "Officer, I don't know if I was speeding or not, but I just placed a 911 call. I'm trying to get home before my husband kills himself."

The officer replied, "I know. We are at the house now. I want to lead you, because we don't want you to run into a dangerous situation."

Wow! The officer pulled ahead of Laura and they both took off!

When they arrived at the house the whole neighborhood was covered with police cars. Laura could count six within her line of sight. An officer in the driveway came over to the car and said that Jeff was not in the house. His truck, however, was in the driveway so they were searching the neighborhood. They took Laura into the house. Two officers remained with her and the rest left for the search. Carla, from the office, showed up and for a lack of knowing what to do to help went straight to the kitchen and started washing dishes. Sherry was also there, but remained in the parking lot across the street. The officers explained to Laura that they really did not know where to look, but they were searching the woods close to the house.

Laura excused herself, went to her bedroom and got down on her knees. She prayed, "Dear Lord, Father of all the Universe, I do not know how to pray or what to pray for in this situation. I do not know what your will is. So, Dear Heavenly Father, please give me the strength and the wisdom to deal with whatever your will is for my family. Please be with the police officers and keep them from harm. In Jesus' name I pray. Amen."

When she returned to the living room she was told that they had an area to search because they had heard a gunshot.

A few minutes later they were notified that they had Jeff and that he was okay. He had been found with the gun in his mouth and they talked him out of pulling the trigger. They were proceeding downtown with him and a lieutenant was coming to the house to speak to her.

Lieutenant Black sat beside Laura on the couch. He explained how serious the situation was. He said that he had never seen a person so close to suicide. Normally, when a person was acting like Jeff acted, they could not save the situation. Jeff had told them that he was shaking so badly that he missed his head with the first shot. He put the gun in his mouth to make sure he did not miss again. They found him in the woods near the path that the neighborhood children would take to the park. Just listening to that part of the conversation made Laura livid.

Lieutenant Black went on to say that he was very concerned about Laura and her sons. He told her that people who do this are very likely to try again. Laura said that this was actually his third attempt. Well, Lieutenant Black felt sure that he would do this again. He said, "Next time, who will try to stop him? Will it be you or one of your boys? Lots of times when that happens innocent people get hurt. Sometimes people just don't want to leave this earth by themselves so they take some people out with them. You need to get away from this man. Your children need to be away from him. He is a dangerous person. Everyday that your children spend away from him will be a day that they will be stronger for it. Now, I need to discuss commitment with you. Jeff needs to be committed for a while. I can do it or you can do it. It does not matter to me. If you decide not to do it, I will and I will also charge him with attempted murder and discharging a firearm within the city limit. It is your choice. But I will tell you this, this man has serious problems and you should not allow him back in this house. Am I making myself clear? You should not allow him back in this house."

Laura understood completely and signed the commitment papers. Everyone left but Carla. Carla eventually went back to the office with the news that Laura would still be at the presentation tomorrow and her children would be in school. They would stay in school until they got upset, but they needed to see that she had confidence in the doctors and that life needed to go on. Laura went to the schools to gather her children. They needed to hear this story from her, first. There was peace and calm in the household that evening.

The next day the presentation went well. David was the first to have trouble at school. Laura left work, picked him and Dylan up and headed home. First thing on the agenda was to look for the dogs. For some reason Jeff had set them free and they had not come home. Laura had an ad in the paper and had called the pound. They rode by the pound just in case. No luck. How cruel.

After forty-eight hours they could see Jeff so they began their daily visits. Jeff was very proud of himself. He sat in the bed reading magazines and fixing his hair. He said that he could not believe that he actually had the nerve to try to kill himself. There were so many people in there that needed help. He was not going to any of the counseling sessions because he was not one of them. Several of the patients were coming to him for help and he was helping them to get their lives in order. Laura was mad as hell, but was at a loss as to what to do.

They could not find the dogs anywhere. They prayed. They prayed for the dogs. They prayed for Jeff. They prayed for themselves. Susan understood what her Dad was going through, but she could not explain it to anyone else.

Easter Sunday was around the corner. Laura found an ad in the paper for some Labs with no papers for $35. She went to see the dogs. The owner thought they were full blooded from the dog next door, but he wasn't sure. Laura sat on the ground close to the dogs. One came up to her and crawled on her lap. The owner said that was unusual because he was very shy. Laura paid for the dog and said that she would be by later. She went to the hospital for another visit. She checked the dog pound one last time. She called Annie to see if she could keep the puppy on her porch overnight. She helped dye eggs for the boys and at last the day was over.

Laura left home long enough to pick up puppy supplies, the puppy, and establish him on Annie's front porch. She returned home to fix supper, lay plans for Easter Sunday, see to the clothes, and get the household to bed. About two AM she returned to Annie's for the dog. She sat him up in the utility room right next to the living room. That way the puppy would hear Susan, David and Dylan the next morning when the Easter baskets were claimed. Then she went to bed. She expected to hear cries from the puppy. She did not. He was either content or she was too exhausted to hear.

The next morning she heard the children. David came to her room to wake her up. He said, "Mom, that puppy was the best thing you could have ever done for Dylan. You should have seen his face when he found him. He wants to name him 'Bucky'." Having the dog turned out later to be the best decision for a lot of people.

On their way home from church Laura realized how bad her brakes were. She had been so busy that it was the first moment she had to even think about something like bad brakes. She also thought about the trip they should make to the hospital and almost got sick on her stomach. They had a nice Easter dinner and Laura made a decision. She did not want to go to the hospital. Just two years ago they had spent Easter Sunday at the mental hospital because of Susan. Now they had a chance to spend another Easter Sunday at another mental hospital because of Jeff. She was afraid that her children would begin to think this was normal. She called the hospital and told Jeff that they were not coming.

Her brakes were too bad too drive and they would see him again as soon as her brakes were fixed. So it was. The family relaxed and enjoyed the day. The next week they were all on vacation. They played with Bucky and had a good time.

On Monday Laura received a call from Jeff's doctor. He was upset by Jeff's attitude. He was not going to any sessions and stayed in his room. Laura relayed some of Jeff's comments. The doctor asked if Laura intended to let him come home. Laura told him what the police officer had said, but she wanted to do what was right for Jeff. She could use help from the doctor. And help she got.

She and the boys were sitting in Jeff's room when the doctor came in. He looked at Jeff and said, "It seems like you have a really nice family here, Mr. McDowell."

"Yes, I do."

"Then it seems like you should be more concerned about what you did to them."

"What do you mean?"

"That's what I mean. You haven't even considered what you have done to them. You haven't even considered what they have been through. You just sit in this room being proud of yourself for acting like a fool. Have you even asked how they were doing?"

"Well, no, but they are doing fine. They would tell me if they weren't."

"Would they now? How are you folks doing?"

Laura said, "Well, actually it's been pretty rough." David said that Dylan had been very upset and he, himself, had to check out of school.

"See, Mr. McDowell, you should be trying to get some help so you won't put them through anything else. Have you thought to ask if this lovely lady will even let you return home after what you did?"

"No."

Everyone turned to Laura. She replied, "Actually, I have been giving it some thought because I've been told by the police and doctors that it would be dangerous for Jeff to come home. I was hoping that things would go better in here."

Jeff looked like he had been kicked in the teeth. He was furious. He almost showed the doctor his real "hate" look, the one where you know he wants you dead, but he held back.

The doctor then said, "Laura, what do you want from Jeff?"

"Well, I'd like for him to participate in the therapy offered here. I'd like for him to take his medication as prescribed."

The doctor said to Jeff, "See? See how close you are to losing your family because you are so selfish? I am going to speak with your psychiatrist. He will talk with Laura and set up a time for you to have some joint counseling. I hope this works for you, Mr. McDowell. I hope you pay attention to what you have done, because it looks like you are getting ready to lose a very loving family. It was a really stupid thing that you did."

Laura knew that Jeff wanted to kill the doctor and her, too. He always had a pure fit if he were criticized in any way. He would just puff up like an old toad and then he would scream and argue for hours. When the doctor left the room, Jeff told Laura and the boys to get the hell out and not come back. That was fine with Laura. She didn't want to be there in the first place.

Late one night the next week the phone rang and it was the hospital. It was not Jeff's hospital. It was the local hospital. Susan had been in a wreck and Laura needed to come to the emergency room. Laura got poor Annie to come stay with the children. At the hospital she found Susan with a slight concussion and a cut eye in need of stitches. Someone had plowed into Susan while she was trying to make a left turn. The car was destroyed. Susan wanted Laura to hold her hand while she had the stitches. Laura was glad to do this. It was the first time Laura ever felt that Susan wanted her around. When they took Susan upstairs to have a CAT scan, Laura went to the waiting room. She picked up the Bible and it opened automatically to Job. She read and read.

Pretty soon Susan was back downstairs. They thought she was fine, but wanted to keep her overnight. Then the police said that they needed to talk to Laura. It seems that drug paraphernalia had been found in Susan's car. They were going to charge Susan and would like for Laura to be present. Wonderful. Susan was charged and given a court date of May $25^{th}$.

There were several more visits to the hospital to work with Jeff and his psychiatrist. The understanding was 1) Jeff was to take his medication as prescribed and only secure a week's worth at a time, 2) Jeff was to continue psychiatric help, and 3) Jeff would have a plan for handling depression. Yeah, right.

Jeff was out of the hospital in less than three weeks. All the right plans were made including doctor's appointments and prescriptions. On the way home Jeff had Laura stop at a doctor's office and told Laura to wait in the car. This was the office of a doctor not involved in Jeff's normal run, although Laura had been there with him once before. When Jeff came out, he had enough pills for an entire month. When Laura asked about it, she was told to shut up. Just shut up!

Once at home, they had a nice supper, one that Jeff actually ate with his family. Then they all went to the sofa to watch some TV. Jeff was getting to know the new puppy. He had no idea what had happened to the other dogs. All of a sudden, Jeff hurled Bucky across the room. Bucky landed with a yelp. Laura ran to him and picked him up. She said, "Why did you do that?"

Jeff replied, "He scratched me, so I threw him."

Laura said, "He's a puppy. Puppies scratch. Don't hold him anymore!" The rest of the family sat there stunned as the evening continued.

The next afternoon in the kitchen Jeff began a conversation about getting the rest of his medication. Laura said, "Jeff, I have to remind you of our agreement in the hospital. You agreed to take your medicine as prescribed and only get a week's worth at a time." He replied, "Well, if it doesn't work this month, that's what I'll do next time."

Laura said, "There will be no next time. We agreed that this time was the only time."

"What do you mean no next time?" Now Jeff had the look, the look of death with the piercing eyes and the curled mouth. He continued, "Are you telling me that if I don't take my medicine right we are through?" Now he was screaming.

Laura said, "Yes, that is exactly what I'm saying." Jeff screamed for her to go to hell. She didn't have to, however, because he left for the garage. Laura was sorry that she had not listened to the lieutenant.

The next day Laura visited the mental health clinic and relayed all the events to her doctor. He told her that she must get away. He said that if she felt like she needed documentation she should buy one of those seven-day pill containers and ask Jeff if he would use it. That way she would know for sure. He said that she needed to do something other than just move out. It was her house, after all. If she had an apartment, Jeff would know where it was because he knew where his children went to school and would follow them home. He did not want to scare Laura, but he felt that her life could be in danger and she needed to take every precaution. She absolutely could not hand him separation papers and stay in the same house. She could not be alone with him when she handed him the papers. She needed to think and to plan.

Laura had talked with Jeff's doctor in Pittsburgh that same morning. This doctor said that there was nothing more he could do for Jeff. She stopped on the way home to pick up the pill case. She asked Jeff if she could speak to him in the back yard. She told him what the doctor said about no more surgery. Then she said, "I bought this pill container for you today. I thought that if you were really serious about trying to take your medicine correctly, this would help. You could fill this up once a week, and then you would know exactly how you stood."

Jeff took the container from Laura's hand. He looked at her with all the hate he could muster and said, "I will not take any ultimatums from you. I no longer consider us man and wife." With that, he threw the pill container at her and stormed back into the house.

Laura sat outside for a few minutes. The decision had been made and she didn't have to be the one to do it. She had said once "Until death us do part". She felt that Jeff's attempted suicide released her from her vows and now, he had said they were no longer man and wife. She knew that it would be her that would die first from his hands. She initiated her plan.

The next day she called her cousin, Daniel, an attorney, to get the name and number of an attorney that handled divorces. She made the next call and got an appointment for the following day. She called her Aunt Cathy to tell her that she and Jeff were going to divorce. Her aunt was absolutely thrilled by the news. Laura started gathering records and was soon able to sneak off from work to see the attorney and fill out form after form after form. She stressed that legal papers needed to be drawn up as fast as possible.

At home things were ice. Jeff rented a bunch of movies and suggested that Laura watch them. In all of the movies, the husband killed the wife.

Jeff announced that he was taking the boys to the beach for the weekend and Laura was not wanted. He made up a story that the boys did not want her to come. Now, Jeff's driving was the world's worst. He was only good for about thirty minutes before he started falling asleep. Laura offered to drive them to the beach and then have Dianne pick her up. That way, he would not have the long drive. No way would he have that. He was taking them and that was all there was to it. Laura was afraid that she would never see her sons again. Would they survive the trip? Would he come back with them or just keep on going? This was the same man that would get lost trying to cross the state of North Carolina when Walker was in the marines. What took most people five hours would take him three days. He would call home from some strange small town to find out where he was and what he should do from there. The attorney said that there was nothing that she could do about it.

Jeff rented some movies that he wanted Laura to watch. On Thursday night he insisted that Laura watch a movie that was just her style. Unfortunately, she got too sleepy and went to bed. Laura's emotions had her completely drained.

She tried again to convince Jeff to let her drive them to the beach. No deal. They were leaving at five the next morning and she was not wanted. Laura stayed up all Friday night to be sure to be able to tell her boys goodbye the next morning. She watched one old movie after another and cried and prayed and cried and prayed. Then they were gone. When David called to say they had made it, Laura took a fitful nap, then went to a movie, *Maverick*, and enjoyed watching James and Mel, her two favorite stars. She went to visit her friend, Vonda, the secretary in their office. Afterwards, Laura called Walker and said that if he would bring his girl over for supper, she would pick up some steaks. Laura had done all she could to make it through the day.

On Sunday she went to church and prayed. She picked up some lunch and decided to watch the movie to see what all the hullabaloo was about. In the movie this lady told her husband that she was having an affair. He hit her and left. When he returned the woman had been beaten up really badly and the police were there. He was arrested. Then she had him committed because he was acting so crazy. One day he phoned her from the institution to tell her that she had forgotten something and he needed to see her. When his wife arrived the man told her that if he killed her, he would be out in a couple of years because people thought he was crazy, but she would be dead forever. Then he choked her to death. Laura had cold chills. She called her friend from yesterday and told her what Jeff had insisted that she watch. She said that she wanted someone to know just in case something happened to her overnight.

When Jeff returned that evening with the boys Laura was overjoyed. As she was changing the sheets in the boys' room, something she felt safe in doing since they were back, Jeff came to the doorway. "Did you get a chance to watch the movie?"

"Well, no, I started watching it, but I didn't think I would like it so I watched something else."

Jeff then told Laura about the movie, leaving out nothing. When he finished, he just stood there and stared at her for a long, long time. Laura finally said, "Well, I'm glad I didn't watch it." He stared some more and left the room.

When Laura went to bed that night she thanked the Lord for the safe return of her children and for the comfort others had supplied her over the weekend. She ended with what was to be her prayer for the next two weeks, "Now I lay me down to sleep. I pray the Lord my soul to keep. If I should die before I wake, I pray the Lord my soul to take."

Monday morning she met with her insurance agent to change her beneficiaries and called her attorney to speed things up. She called her sister to discuss where she should go. She called school principals to see when David and Dylan would be through with end-of grade tests and would it be possible for them to miss the last ten days or so of school. She was thinking and planning but was very scared. She talked with her boss to make sure everybody understood how serious things were. He gave her permission to put whatever she needed in the supply closet. She couldn't store anything in her office, because everything needed to appear normal.

Laura had some small IBM bags that she would carry back and forth to work. They had been holding the current project, but not anymore. She would take them home almost empty, but when she came to work in the mornings she would have an outfit for Dylan or David or some important papers. Sometime she would sneak some of her own clothes. She went to the drug store and bought toothbrushes, toothpaste, necessary toiletries. She even thought to buy dog food, dog bowls, anything she could think of.

Finally, the call came from her attorney that she could pick up the papers in two days. She called her sister. Dianne wanted them to stay with her but Laura would not do it because it was the first place Jeff would look. She made an appointment with her doctor. She called the principals. She called her friend, Tonya, who had agreed to help her. She went to the police station.

On May 22nd, Laura kept her doctor's appointment. She was very nervous. When her doctor asked how she was, she told him. After the exam, he wrote her a note to be excused from work for ten days and also gave her a prescription for some nerve pills. She went to the attorney and picked up the papers. When she returned to work, Jeff called. He said that he was fixing a good supper. He wanted to have a nice evening because for some reason he felt like he was losing his family. Laura would really have to be careful.

There was a strange calmness for Laura on the morning of the twenty-third. David knew, but Dylan did not, what was about to happen. As with most mornings, Jeff did not move off the sofa until time for them to leave. Laura said to David, "We have some extra things to do this morning. See that garbage bag of stuff on the steps? It's for the Salvation Army. How about putting it in the car for me? And, remember you were told that you could bring the ferrets for show and tell this week. I think that today would be the day since your class went to the zoo yesterday. Put them in the car too." Everybody brushed their teeth and got in a pretty full car. As soon as the car was started, Laura said to David, "Grab Bucky and be quick about it." They were off!

The first stop was Tonya's house. Her daughter was home from college and was to keep an eye on David and Dylan. Laura unloaded the children and pets and headed to work. She gave her boss the note from her doctor and repacked the car. Then she headed for the police station.

Sergeant Tallent was a massive man. He listened to every word Laura said. He was told about the craziness, Jeff's Marine background, and the fear that she had. He told her not to worry. Laura left the police station with two police escorts. One officer was already there, in the parking lot.

Sergeant Tallent and another officer went into the house with Laura. Of course Jeff was in a total panic. Laura asked him to sit down so she could explain. The police did not take their eyes off of Jeff. Laura said, "Jeff these are legal separation papers."

"What?! Why are you doing this?!"

"I have to do this, Jeff. I do not feel safe. You are not seeing a psychiatrist. You will not take your medicine correctly. You said that we were no longer man and wife. I know you want to see David and Dylan as soon as possible. I am giving you a check from my mother's account for $1000. Please use it to find a place to live and get settled. If you need to sell the old Camaro that you bought for David, please do. Also please leave enough money in our account for me to make the house payment. Susan graduates on June 2. I would like for you to stay until that happens so her life will not be interrupted any more than necessary. Please be out of the house within two days after that. One other thing, your children will come back to this house. I don't care what you take, but please leave it in some kind of order for them to return to."

"Can I have another chance?"

"I'm sorry, Jeff, this was your last chance." And they left.

Sergeant Tallent followed Laura to Tonya's and waited until the car was all set. Then he followed them to the county line. Dylan still had not grasped the situation. He thought they were going to the beach for a few days until Dad got better. And that was the destination. Laura did not follow the normal path because she did not want Jeff catching up with them if he was of that mind. She stopped about halfway and called Susan at school. She told Susan what she had done and what she had said to Jeff about graduation and moving out. She told Susan that she should not expect her Dad to be in a good mood, if he remembered to pick her up after school at all. She told Susan that she was sorry about how things had worked out, wished her luck in court and for graduation, told her she loved her, and got off the phone.

Laura made it to Wilmington and checked into the motel where Dianne had made the reservations. Dianne and Charles came over. Charles listened with amazement at the story. They took the ferrets and Bucky to their house. Then everybody met for dinner. By this time Laura was really anxious and her stomach was giving her a fit. Still, it was a good time for David and Dylan so she tried to relax. When they returned to the motel the boys fell asleep watching TV while Laura unpacked what little they had and set the coolers right. The last thing to unpack was the plastic bag that David put in the car. It contained all the cool stuff that would have been missed if packed ahead of time. After all, you can't spend ten days at the beach without roller blades, helmets, bathing suits, and games to play!

David and Dylan would sleep through the motel breakfast, but Laura would go down and bring cereal and fruit back to the room. She would drink coffee and read and think until they woke up. Some days they would head for the beach and some days the pool. Some times they would have a sandwich in the room and sometimes fast food. They would check on the pets. A few times they ate supper with Dianne and Charles. Once, when it was raining so bad that the streets were flooded, Laura had to place a takeout order from the very expensive restaurant next door and go pick it up, on foot, without a raincoat. The water was just about to her knees in some places. She took the boys to a bicycle shop and let them each pick out a bike. They spent several afternoons on bike trails in the next county. Laura would sit in the car and read while the boys would ride. When the car needed CV joints they spent the day at the mall and the movie while the car was being fixed. When Dianne could get off work they would go to a different beach or take the jet skis out into the waterway and ocean. Dianne and Dylan would ride on one with Laura and David on the other.

Only once did a bad thing happen. Dylan got choked on an ice cube. Laura was trying to follow the first aid rules that she did not know very well. Just the slinging around of Dylan was enough to dislodge anything that was lodged. David said that he hoped he never had to go through anything like that. It was funny when it was over, but Laura realized just how close to the edge she was.

Jeff called Dianne once to see if they were there. Laura was glad that Dianne could say that they were not.

Strange, but Laura never took a nerve pill. She never went back to Alanon. She felt such peace. Praise the Lord.

When Laura saw that *Mrs. Doubtfire* was coming on TV she knew that it was time to tell Dylan that she and his Dad had separated. It was pretty tough. Dylan got upset for a few minutes. Laura assured him that he would have time with his Dad, probably more time and certainly quality time that he had not had before. They watched the movie, talked some more, said their prayers and went to bed.

Laura felt very badly for hurting Dylan. After the boys were asleep she went over in her mind all of the events that led up to separation. To her there had been no choice. She hoped that some day Dylan would understand.

They headed home on Sunday, one day before Jeff was to be out of the house. Dianne came too. The Buffett concert was scheduled for Monday night and Laura was in possession of four tickets. They went to the river cabin to spend the night. Even though the house looked like it was vacant, Laura did not want to sleep there until the locks were changed.

Monday was pretty eventful. They checked out the house. It wasn't too bad. One bedroom was empty and the den furniture was gone. The new TV was gone and of course all the tapes and stereo. Dishes and pots and pans were gone but Laura did not care because Jeff was gone. They would be fine. They changed the locks and Laura called an alarm company to come install an alarm.

David wanted to be with his friends rather than to go to the concert so Laura delivered him into the hands of Teresa with strict instructions of what to do in case Jeff showed up. Dianne talked Allen, their cousin, into going with them to the concert. The concert left nothing to be desired. Buffett fans would all understand. Non-Parrot heads would never understand. Everyone stayed up half the night talking. Allen could not spend the night because the sofa was gone. By daybreak Allen left and Dianne and Laura felt secure enough to go to bed.

Dianne left the next morning. Laura checked in with her friend, Di. She also checked the bank accounts to discover that hers was empty and the house payment had not been made. Then she discovered that Dylan's account had been emptied. More than five hundred dollars of birthday, Christmas, and allowance money repurposed to serve a very selfish man. Laura scrambled to get the house payment covered. It was the only time in twenty years that it had been late. It would take four years before the bank took it off their records. She spent some time closing accounts and opening others. The next morning she went back to work to begin her new life.

# Survival

Over the next three years it was up to Laura to make a go of her new life. She was not looking for it to be easy, but at least possible. She had been through some tough times before and she called on those same forces to see her through again.

She bought a welcome mat and opened her house for David and Dylan's friends. She had a long talk with the preacher. For that first summer, she made arrangements to work half-days for the weeks that David and Dylan were not with their dad. Most days she was back home before they were awake enough to want food. She set about making ends meet.

It was a wonderful summer. When she got home from work they would have a meal and plan for the rest of the day. Sometimes they would go to the neighborhood pool across the street. Sometimes they would head to the river for the afternoon. They played with their friends, raced BMX and went to church. Laura talked and visited with relatives; some she had not been able to see since she and Jeff had married.

The house was a mess. She figured that it would take ten years to undo everything that had been done badly. She started with the boys' rooms.

They could finally have their own rooms. She let them pick out the colors and she started painting.

Jeff came to see the boys. Laura was scared. A couple of the guys from work were riding by every few minutes, as were the police. When it didn't look like Jeff was making any plans to leave Di came from down the street. She had been watching from her back door. She said, "If we are going to pick out some carpet for David's room, we need to get going." Jeff was stomping around saying, "What's more important, carpet or a father?" Finally he took his leave. Laura actually found carpet remnants for both rooms for $50 each.

Laura and Jeff went to Mediation to set up custody and visitation. This was very difficult but they could have never done it on their own. Laura was really glad to have someone in the room with her when she was with Jeff. Normally, he was late.

Once it was settled, it was still touch and go because Jeff really believed that rules were for everyone but him. He was always late coming and going. Laura feared for her children's lives when they were with their Dad because he was still mostly stoned. David would always ride in the front seat to help keep his Dad awake and to help watch the road. His apartment was about an hour away. Susan lived there too for a month or so and moved out. Once, Jeff let Dylan play with the gun that he had tried to kill himself with. He gave the boys beer. They had to go back to Mediation to get some things straight.

Their old boat was too much for Laura. It was always broken and it was impossible to load and unload. There was no way Laura could pay to have it stored at a marina so she sold it to her mechanic for $1500. Robert could only afford $700 so Laura took that with the rest coming in payments. She replaced the $500 in Dylan's savings account that Jeff had taken and spent the rest on clothes and school supplies for fall.

She borrowed money from Dianne and bought a used jet ski. David wrecked it the first time out, but once Laura had the part, he also fixed it.

Laura, David, and Dylan took the boating safety course. You had to be sixteen to drive a jet ski on Lake Wylie or you had to be fourteen with the Boating Safety course and test passed. Dylan fussed a little at having to do this, but Laura said that he might as well take the class with them. That way he would have it when he needed it. They all passed. Dylan did as well as David! The instructors and, of course, Laura were very impressed with Dylan. And what do you know, the next summer the rules changed on Lake Wylie and all you needed to drive a jet ski was to be sixteen or pass the test. Laura would not let Dylan leave the cove, but he was very proud of himself.

The day before school started that year, David was bringing the ski up to the marina for Laura to load and Dylan was riding behind him. Laura was on the dock talking to a reporter from Channel Eight. They were doing a story on boating safety. Laura told him about the boating course. Before it was over, they were filming David and Dylan showing all the safety precautions. They were on TV that night. What a way to end the summer!

David road his bike to and from school. Dylan stayed after school in a program for an hour a day until Laura could pick him up. He didn't much care for this, but Laura could not take on the worry of having him walk by himself or be home alone. Both boys made good grades and enjoyed their friends. During the week they would race bikes. On the weekends they would be with their Dad or doing something fun with family and friends. Life was good. Life was peaceful.

Money was pretty tight because Jeff was not paying his part of the bankruptcy or giving any money towards the support of David and Dylan. Because he was on disability, Social Security was sending a check for $411 a month. That was great, but it was not enough. Laura began tutoring to make ends meet. At twenty-five dollars an hour, she could bring in about $400 a month. She could count this as the house payment or as half the bankruptcy payment; whichever meant the most at the time.

Jeff was fighting her on every issue. He was after her retirement, money from the house, even alimony (what?!?). He had a pit bull of an attorney who had just practiced all of this on his ex-wife. Laura could not get Jeff to reason at all. It was like Jeff thought that if he made her miserable enough, she would come back to him. Not likely. The only pleasant time in the year and a half that it took to settle was seeing the expression on Jeff's attorney's face when Laura told him that the house was in her name and she had lived in it for seven years before she and Jeff were married. Laura told Jeff that if he took her to court that she would never forgive him. He did not listen and she never chose to forgive him.

Jeff was to pick David and Dylan up at 11:30 AM for the week before Christmas. That was set so Laura could work for half a day and be home to tell them goodbye during lunch. Jeff showed up at 7:30 AM, ten minutes after Laura had left for work. When David opened the door Jeff came storming in, pushing his way past David. He was yelling, "Where is he? Where is Cooper?" David told him that he had no idea what he was talking about. Jeff replied, "Your mother is having an affair with someone named Cooper. Where is he? I have already been to Annie's to tell her that your mother is having an affair with this Cooper." So, Jeff had already been to Annie's before 7:30 to tell her about someone who didn't exist. Jeff ran all through the house looking for Cooper. When he could not find him, he gathered the boys, their bags and put them in the car for Christmas.

Laura was in a big meeting at the Country Club. She got a message from David saying that their Dad had picked them up and he would call her as soon as he got a chance.

Laura went home at lunch just in case David would call. He did. He asked if she knew anyone named Cooper. When Laura said, "No", David told her about how Jeff had acted that morning. Laura was very concerned for her children. She could make neither heads nor tails of what David was saying. She asked, "Are you at your Dad's?"

"No, we are at some doctor's office in Charlotte."

"What?"

"We have been here all morning, sitting in the waiting room. We are really bored."

"Do you know the name of this doctor?"

"No, but we have been here before. You were here too." When David described the office, Laura knew exactly where they were. Jeff had been there before to get drugs. He had promised Laura that he was going there to ask for some treatment to get off the drugs and take something else, but when they got in the office, he asked for drugs instead. When the doctor left the room Laura questioned Jeff's decision. She was told to shut up. This was one of the doctors who said that it was amazing that they were still together.

Laura spoke very seriously to David. She said that she was very concerned. She said that the only person she could think of named Cooper was the man that James Garner had played in "*Maverick*." She figured that Jeff was hallucinating the rest. It was well known that Laura was a James Garner fan and she had seen Jeff hallucinate before. Anyway, she was going to get off the phone and try to talk to the doctor. She told David that she loved him and to please call whenever they made it to their Dad's.

Laura dialed the number for the doctor's office. When a lady answered the phone she explained who she was and asked her to look across the room to verify her two children were sitting there. She said, "I realize that you cannot tell me anything about a patient and one of your doctors, but I believe that my ex-husband is in your office for the sole purpose of getting drugs. I am very concerned about my children. They have been sitting there all morning. Jeff was not supposed to pick them up until about this time. I am also concerned that he is going to receive drugs and be driving with my children in his car."

The nurse replied, "Just a moment, please."

Laura waited for what seemed an eternity. When the nurse came back on the line she said, "You are correct in that we cannot discuss a patient with you. However, no one in the care of those two children will be leaving our office with drugs today." Laura got down on her knees and prayed. Obviously, the nurse had gotten to the doctor in time.

Laura called her attorney and was told that until Jeff actually hurt one of his children, there was nothing that could be done.

It was after supper before Laura heard from David again. He said that his Dad was real mad when they left the office. Laura asked to speak to Jeff. She did not mention the drugs, but she did mention Cooper. She asked where Jeff had heard such a thing. He said that he couldn't remember and he realized that it was not true. He could not explain why he had done what he did.

And Jeff was wondering why she wouldn't give him a second chance.

The boys were back on Christmas Eve. Laura was ready. They had a great Christmas and a great week following.

Then on a trip to the river cabin, Laura discovered that a tree limb had fallen from a giant oak tree, gone through the roof and punctured a hole in the bedroom ceiling. Thank goodness she had taken out more insurance. The insurance, however, would only pay for half a roof and the whole thing was in bad need of repair. It also already had a rolled roof put on by Laura and Dianne and a shingle roof put on by Laura and Jeff. Robert, the mechanic who purchased the boat, had always offered to work on the cabin in trade for some time to relax there, so Laura approached him with a deal. The boys were to spend the week of the Fourth of July with their Dad. Robert said that he and one of his friends would replace the roof for free if they could stay the week in the cabin and consider the boat paid for. Laura agreed.

Now, she was sitting at home, alone, during the week of the fourth. She had never done this before. She had always been at the river or at the beach. Plus, she did not have her boys with her. It was pretty miserable even if she was working most days. To top it all off she kept hearing the commercials about the summer Olympics. For a meager $700 per person you could go to the Olympics and see one event and fly home. That seemed a bit steep to Laura so she called the airlines and discovered that a round-trip ticket from Charlotte to Atlanta was only $138. Then she called to check on the prices for the events. They ranged from $10 to $650 depending on what you wanted to see. Hummmmm. By the end of the day Laura had booked three seats on a flight and bought tickets to the field hockey event for $10 each and the judo event for $40 each. Judo was more expensive because the medals would be presented, but it would be worth the price. She figured that by the time they ate she would have spent her entire teaching supplement in one day and, of course, began to worry if she had made a mistake. It was set for July $21^{st}$, her fiftieth birthday, and although she was sure they deserved it, she was still a little surprised at herself.

She called Dianne to tell her what she had done, expecting Dianne to fuss at her about the money. Dianne said, "Brad has been so upset with me because we are not going when we live so close. Would you mind if we got tickets too and went with you?"

And they did. Dianne and Brad came to Laura's on Saturday where they had a full-blown birthday celebration. The next morning they flew to Atlanta where they thoroughly enjoyed the day and flew back home. It was the first time David and Dylan had been on a jet. The whole adventure was something that they would all remember for a long, long time. It was a day later that the bomb went off in the trashcan right where they had been standing.

The school year progressed nicely. David was working some in the afternoons. Laura was painting, repairing, and tutoring. Dylan was enjoying himself.

David was about to turn fifteen. For his birthday, he had invited about twenty people to a biking party and cookout at the track. It was all set for Sunday. When all the shopping was done, Laura decided to go by the nursing home to see her Mom.

When she arrived, the nurse told Laura that her mother was not doing well. Laura tried to get her to explain exactly what that meant, but did not get very far. Her mom had not spoken in six months. All she could get from the nurse was that her mother was not responding and had not eaten. Laura stayed for a while and left to check on the boys.

After dinner Laura was making the final preparations for the party when the phone rang. It was the nursing home again saying that Laura should return. Laura called Annie to come be with the boys and left.

At the nursing home she tried again to get some information. Finally, she asked to use the phone to call Dianne. She looked at one nurse and asked, "Should I tell my sister to drive here from Wilmington tonight or wait until the morning?"

This nurse said, "Tell her to come tonight."

Then Laura knew. She called Vonda, her friend from work. Vonda picked up David and Dylan and brought them to the nursing home. Her cousin, Walter, drove up from Charlotte to keep her company until Dianne arrived.

Dianne got there about 4 AM. And Walter went home. Laura's mom had been moved to another room. The boys alternated from the waiting room to the new room. Dianne and Laura stayed by their Mom until the end. At eight-thirty Laura said a prayer asking the Lord to be with her Mom. At eight thirty-two, her mother was gone.

Dianne and Laura had to wait for the details and the funeral home. While all of this was going on, they discussed David's birthday party. They would not be needed at the funeral home until Monday and cousins were making the necessary phone calls. Grandmaw had always loved birthdays. They reminisced about their parties in the back yard with the fancy hats their Mom had made and the sleepovers at the river and in their living room. They decided to go on with the party. They figured it was what their Mom would have wanted.

Except for the fact that Laura really did not know what she was doing, it was a very successful party. Only one child was hurt on the track, but his mom was there to take care of him.

The day of the funeral Jeff showed up and pretended to be a member of the family. He had not once visited Laura's Mom in the nursing home. After the service he came to Laura's and proceeded to take David out to celebrate his birthday. Dylan and Susan went also. It was okay because there was plenty to eat at Laura's and she had some time to visit with Dianne, Charles, and her nephews.

David was saving his money like mad to buy a car. He was still working in the afternoons and baby-sitting Dylan. Laura adjusted her work schedule to get him to work and have plans for Dylan. She took two weeks vacation and painted the outside of her house and the outside of the river cabin. She covered the nine different colors that Jeff had left on her house with beige and cream. What a relief. What an accomplishment. In the fall she began her training with Novell. It consumed all of her spare time for a year.

David bought a car he found on the Internet. He got his driver's license. Laura studied for her Novell Network Instructor Certification. Dylan played.

The summer of '98 was a great summer. On the weekends they went to the river and visited Dianne in Wilmington. Once they went to Hilton Head Island because Laura had agreed to listen to a Time-Share spiel. That was all she had agreed to so that's all she did. She was getting use to playing this game. They took the "Fireworks and Dinner" cruse on her birthday. During the day they dug up sand dollars with their toes while swimming in the ocean. Peace and wonderment filled Laura's life. Praise the Lord.

# Alex Returns

Things seemed to be falling into place. School had started without a hitch. David and Dylan were content with their courses, and for the most part, the friends that were in their classes. Once again, Dylan did not get some of the teachers he wanted, and it looked like it would be another year without David Anderson in his class. Still, Laura knew that the important things were running very smoothly. Everyone was healthy. David picked Dylan up each afternoon and brought him safely home. The speeding ticket and pot use of last winter seemed to be a thing of the past. Guys still hung around in the driveway and filled up the garage with abandoned chairs to make themselves more at home. There were no drugs, but there were cigarettes and new girl friends. David had a new job at Food Lion, new wheels for his car, and a new girl friend named Beverly. Beautiful girl. College bound.

Laura's Novell pathway was almost finished, just a few more forms to fill out. The paint was still on the house and the roof was not leaking. The river cabin still wanted for some fixing, but it would have to wait for a cooler month. The end of August is no time to work outside even if you can go jump in a lake. Dylan was contemplating a river cabin birthday party on Sept. 20th. Any painting would certainly have to wait until after that momentous occasion. It had been a grand summer and there was no end in sight.

It was the Wednesday before Labor Day when the phone rang. Laura was in the living room with the boys and closest to the phone. "Hello," she answered.

"Laura, this is Alex from Charlotte. Do you remember me?"

Laura's heart skipped several beats and there was no telling what havoc was happening to other bodily functions. Good Lord, it was Alex from the past. Who would have ever thought? What was this all about and where was Ann, his wife, and the competition from days of old? And why was he calling after, what, twenty years? Now what, one of the most honest guys she had ever dated was on the other end of the phone. This guy was smart and funny and safe, no doubt about being afraid to be with him, so what the hell was going on and why was he calling? Maybe he was looking for someone else, probably was, what do you say, and in front of David and Dylan? "Yes, of course I do. Could you hold for a minute and let me change phones?" "David, hang this up when I get to the bedroom."

"Okay I'm back."

"I was going through my list of old friends and I ran across Jayne's name. I talked to her the other day and she said I should give you a call. She said you were separated from Jeff. Is this true?"

"Yes. We separated three years ago in June. Where is Ann?

"Ann and I separated in '93, but we kept seeing each other and living in the same house for awhile. I can't believe you've been separated that long. Are you divorced?"

"Yes. It will be two years in October. Are you? What happened?"

"Well, I don't know. I'm not sure I should have married Ann in the first place. It just slowly fell apart. I built this great big house for us and I ended up on the second floor and she stayed on the first. Then we just kept living like that until I finally wised up."

"That's very strange, Alex. Where was the kitchen?"

"On her floor."

"Did you have pass through rights or did you have to climb in a window?"

"Most of the time I could pass through. Sometimes I couldn't use the kitchen. You know, I talked to Jayne more than once, but when I talked to her before she said that Jeff was sick, but that you were very happy."

"There is a problem there because Jayne and I didn't really see each other for about ten years. Actually, I didn't see anyone. Everyone thought we were real happy, but the truth is that Jeff was stoned and I was miserable. I kept thinking he would get better so I kept hanging in there. I knew that once the bad outweighed the good, I would be gone, but I had a hard time giving up. I really wanted the marriage to work but it kept getting worse and worse. Finally, when I thought he was going to kill me, I knew I could end it. But that's another story."

"When I talked to Jayne last she told me you might need some help. Any chance of our getting together for a visit? Maybe we could go out to dinner."

"Alex, you don't want to take me anywhere."

"Why?"

"Because I'm old and fat. I don't ever do anything, so I doubt I would be much fun."

"Well, let me be the judge of that. We can always be friends. We always have been friends. Can I at least call you and talk to you again on Monday? Maybe we can make some plans for next week. I'm going up to see your friend and mine, Al Davis, this weekend."

"Okay, call me Monday. We are going to spend this weekend at the river."

"All right, but I'll call tomorrow. I'm glad you still have the river cabin. Remember the time you drug my ass out there in the middle of the night to look for that ring you lost? Did you ever find it?"

"Yes. One day I found it in the driveway. It was in pretty good shape considering the lawn mower ran over it. In fact, I have it on right now."

The ring was one of the last presents Laura had received from her father and probably meant more to her than any other piece of jewelry ever could.

"Okay. We'll talk tomorrow. If you need to get in touch with me, I'm in the phone book. It's Shuford on Landis Drive. Oh, tell me one thing, is your hair short or is it still long and brown?"

"It's still long and brown."

"Thank God. Talk to you on Monday."

Laura hung up the phone in total shock. The possibilities of this situation were mind boggling. Alex Shuford. I'll be damned. What had prompted this, and what was to be done? No, dating someone was out of the question. Where would she find the time and what would the kids think? They really needed some extended, uninterrupted stability after all the turmoil and chaos of their father and the divorce. Still, since the Novell courses were almost finished, some time should be freeing up. Laura went to the mirror for the painful look-see. It was painful all right; sitting around studying for a year had really left its mark. How could anyone be interested in this rotund person? The face was okay, very few wrinkles for fifty-two. Well, not the time to think about this now, better to get back to the boys and check on the homework and make sure everyone had clothes to wear tomorrow.

Labor Day weekend left too much time for Laura to think about Alex. The weekend started off very badly with very bad car brakes. The noise, the unique "no brake pad" groan, started up as soon as Laura picked up Dylan's friend for the weekend trip. By the time they got home it was unbearable. What a downer. All packed and can't go. David and his friend, Chris, went to work. Three hours later, two trips to the store, and around the corner to get advice and tools from Jim, the job was done. Pretty good for two teenagers. The one thing going right in this world for Laura was her precious and industrious sons. Never would she forget to be thankful for such fine young men. So the trip was delayed a few hours, but now it was a beautiful Saturday afternoon and Laura was sitting on the deck listening to Willie Nelson's Stardust tape and mulling over the possibilities with Alex. The real kicker here was that she would have to date someone for a year before she knew as much about them as she already knew about Alex. And it was a known fact that she could never trust a stranger, would never date a stranger, or give them a chance to hurt her anymore.

Laura met Alex through dating Al Davis. Al had been kind enough to take her out after the fisticuffs. It didn't go well with Al, but Al had taken her to Alex's to meet him. Ann, Alex's girlfriend, went to sleep on the sofa shortly after they arrived. Alex did not seem to mind and the three of them stayed up most of the night telling jokes and in general having a really fine time. Laughing hard enough to cry does not happen often. It was even later that through another friend, Steve, that Alex knew she was interested. Ann seemed to come and go out of the picture, but always hanging around as some sort of competition. The problem with competition at this stage of Laura's life was all the women who had competed with her for Keith's affection during her first marriage. Keith never held anything back from anyone except Laura. Anyway, there was Ann, pretty, blond and eight years younger than Laura. Laura would not even begin to compete with her after Keith. Alex did not want another family. Why should he with two little girls? Laura eventually let go to find that pie in the sky relationship. She remembered that Alex actually looked serious the day they parted. She could still see his eyes. Maybe he would miss her and maybe not. For sure, he would be able to fill up his time with a large assortment of females waiting in the wings, just looking for a handsome, unattached college graduate. But Alex never said anything about his feelings for Laura. So, other than some loudly speaking actions, there was nothing to go on. Off she went. She married Jeff. Alex married Ann. Eighteen years passed.

Laura headed to the phone book. Yep, there it was, just as he said. She listened for the sound of the beep and said, "Alex, this is Laura. I've been thinking about this meeting thing and Dylan will be at a party on Monday and David has to work. Maybe we could set this up for then, if you don't have plans. Then you will know if you want to spend any more time with this little, old, fat woman, and I'll know if I should stop listening to this Willie Nelson album. Give me a call."

She picked the phone up and dialed again. "Alex, I don't mean to scare you too much about this fat thing. I can still water-ski, so I guess it can't be all that bad."

The next twenty days in Laura's life were magical indeed. The first meeting with Alex went very well. There was so much to catch up on; it didn't look like it could all ever be covered, especially on a beautiful September afternoon. Alex had not changed very much in eighteen years, same blue eyes, sharp wit, concern for family, and a little devilish aurora of what could be made out of what had not been.

It was Laura's intention to spend some time with Alex before breaking the news to the boys. The last thing she felt they needed was the ups and downs of a new relationship when their little lives had already been so rocky.

One afternoon Laura remarked to Dylan, "You know what, Hon? Things are going so well it almost scares me. I'm always afraid something bad will happen. I have my little list made out and if things continue, I'll be a CNI and have the kitchen painted in less than a month. Then I'll only have my room to paint. Maybe that can be done by Thanksgiving."

Laura thought back to the week before Thanksgiving six years ago when Jeff came into the bedroom with a bucket of white paint. "What are you going to do?" she asked.

"I'm going to paint this room." He replied.

"Please don't start painting now; it won't get finished before Christmas." Nothing Jeff ever started got finished. At this point the outside of the house still had nine different colors on it.

"I'll have it done by Thanksgiving." And he proceeded to paint the door and part of a wall.

That was it. It never did get finished. Laura left it to last because no one ever saw it but her. Dianne had seen it, but Dianne knew Laura would get to it in good time.

So September continued to be a month of big plans. Laura and Alex went out to dinner twice. It was nice. It was romantic. It was platonic. Laura lost weight. She bought new underwear. She wore her hair straight because Alex liked it that way. It was an amazing feeling to be safe, to be out. Alex told her that he didn't stop dreaming about her until he had been married to Ann for five years. He had all the records they listened to in a box and he would not let Ann get her hands on it. After five years he finally fell in love with Ann and after ten years the marriage was over.

"Why did you marry Ann?" Laura inquired, not knowing if she should be asking, and not knowing if she really wanted to know.

"I don't know. I felt obligated because she was so young and I had slept with her. I called the wedding off right before it was suppose to happen. I don't think Ann's mother ever forgave me, but there was just too much planned and I wanted something simple. Finally, sometime later, I told Ann we could get married if we got married that weekend and went away to do it." was the answer Alex gave. "Anyway, Laura, I never ran around on my wife, I never hit a woman, and I never took drugs."

What was more important was what ended the marriage. According to Alex, Ann's parents would not let them be, especially her mother. Ann drank all the time, did not ever fix or want dinner, and in general turned out to be somewhat of a shallow machine that cried all the time.

Laura shared some of her marriage with Alex. He had trouble comprehending everything she was saying and expressed surprise that Laura would put up with all that. It just didn't seem like the Laura he knew.

Alex remembered everything they had done.

Wednesday nights were still reserved for the church group. This little group added so much sanity to life. It was the first time Laura had ever had the opportunity to really know a preacher and his family. Along with Ben and Margaret there was Wesley and Sally, Al and Jane, Dwight, Cathy, and several others. Most remained constant and were there for every meeting, some came and went. It was very interesting to read the Bible, talk about the lessons, and openly discuss problems. On several occasions, the group had prayed for Laura's family, as they had the rest of the families and other people with needs. They had been there for Laura last spring when the financial settlement knocked the props out from under her. On one of these Wednesday nights, Laura decided to share the news of Alex with Margaret. "I intend to see him several times before I let the boys know I'm dating anyone. I need to know if there is a chance for anything to come of it before I spring this on David and Dylan. I don't want to upset them over nothing. I need to make sure this relationship has a chance."

Margaret looked stunned. After a few minutes, she said, "Laura, I need to let you know that I have been praying for someone to come into your life. I asked the Lord to send someone who would be good to you and take care of you. You are always so strong for the boys; I just wanted someone for you to lean on. Now, I hope I did the right thing. Is he a Christian?"

"Yes. He is from a Christian family, too. Thank you, Margaret. I had not prayed for anyone for myself. I wasn't even looking."

"Please let me know if everything goes all right. I will be worried, but I will trust in the Lord to answer my prayers."

All went as planned until Jeff backed out on his weekend commitment to Dylan. It was not unusual for Dad to cancel plans, but it was most unusual for Laura to have two nights committed to Alex when he did. Now it was decision time. There was no way to see Alex without David and Dylan getting wind of it. There was no way Laura ever wanted the boys to think that she had deceived them in any way. So it was big news time. She called the boys in from the garage.

"We have to have a meeting. I need to tell you something because I do not ever want you to think that I did anything behind your back, I love you too much."

After just a moment's hesitation she began, "Both of you know that I was seeing friends this weekend. I was not worried about you because, Dylan, you were going to be with your Dad, and, David, you had plans for Friday and Saturday night. What I want you to know is that one of the friends I will be seeing this weekend is not a female. His name is Alex Shuford. I knew him and dated him before your Dad and I got married. He lives in Charlotte, has his own business, and graduated from Carolina. I had not mentioned this before because I wanted to spend enough time with Alex to know if it was worth mentioning and taking a chance on upsetting you. Alex is asking me out and I think it is nice for me to be with an adult every now and then. What do you think?"

David said, "I don't see anything wrong with it."

Dylan started to cry.

David went back outside.

"Dylan, tell me what about this bothers you so?" Laura asked as she wrapped her arms around Dylan. Her heart was beginning to break, too.

"Is he going to move in with us? I don't want some stranger living here and I don't want to have to go live with Dad", was his reply.

"Okay, now listen up. No one is going to move in here, especially some stranger. The only way anyone would ever move in here would be if we were married, and you need to rest assured that I'm not going to marry some stranger. If anything ever got that far, it would be years from now, you would be friends and know each other very well. Is that all you are worried about?"

"Yes."

"Well then, quit worrying. All I'm doing is spending some time with an old friend that happens to be a male rather than a female. Are we okay on this? You know, I would never do anything to hurt you or be dishonest with you in any way."

"Yes, I'm okay", Dylan replied slowly. Laura could see he was still in deep thought.

"All right, then, go on back outside and be active. I know you've had a double whammy. I love you."

"I love you, too."

Dylan left the room. Laura cried. In a few minutes David came back in. "Are you sure you're okay with this?" Laura inquired

"Yes, I'm sure."

"Well, then, will you do what you can to help me with Dylan?"

"Sure, we already are. Beverly's parents are divorced. She is talking to us about your being happy. Everybody will be okay."

"Thanks, Hon. Who loves you?"

"You do."

"You got that right."

David gave his mom a hug and went back outside. Laura thought about how lucky she was to have such fine sons. It was a true blessing. Each day she prayed for guidance. All she wanted was for them to continue down the path they were on.

Dylan decided to have his birthday party at the river cabin. He wanted ten of his friends to spend the night and ride the Jet Ski. It was the dickens to organize. They were to go out Friday night after supper, have ice cream and cake, spend the night, have breakfast, and return after lunch. Each parent had to be contacted to see exactly what each child had permission to do. Extra life jackets needed to be rounded up, and food carefully planned. Everything needed to be there. There would be no running to the store and leaving ten thirteen year olds by themselves.

In the midst of the planning, Walker volunteered to help out on Saturday. Alex volunteered to help set up on Friday and take down on Sunday.

Alex met Laura at the cabin Friday for late lunch and decorating. It was nice to sit on the deck and dock and talk and visit and plan. In fact, the visiting caused a real push to get the decorating done in time. There was nothing quite like the river cabin. It was small, so small, that the one air conditioning unit would cool the entire place. There were two bedrooms, the largest being ten by twelve. In that room alone, there were two twin beds, a set of bunk beds and two dressers. It was a tight squeeze at best, but doable. The other bedroom held a queen-size bed and dresser. The room was the same length as the bed. All windows and beds were covered with repurposed covers and curtains from home. Laura had no idea where the boys would want to sleep, but she felt sure she had the small bedroom. There was also a living room with an old kitchen table in it. The entire area was about ten by twenty. The kitchen had once been a small porch. Now there was a larger porch, a bathroom, and a deck. The deck had been done in two doses, one before Hugo and one after. As Alex and Laura were finishing up, Laura, standing much too close to Alex, said, "I guess on Sunday I will have to seduce you."

Alex held Laura gently by the shoulders. He looked straight into her eyes. "You already have," was the reply.

The birthday party was the best ever. Kids everywhere! Splashes everywhere! Hotdogs, cold drinks, ice cream, cake, hundreds of donuts, Jet Ski rides, inner tubes, sleeping bags, all night talking and game playing. A gala affair and another good time had by all!

When Jeff picked Dylan up Sunday for his part of the birthday celebration, Laura headed back to the cabin to clean and see Alex. It appeared that the relationship might even linger longer than their first attempt. In fact, it could possibly last forever. Who knows? Who knows anything about relationships nowadays? Both of these people had severe battle scars, both were well over the romance stage, both were secure in their present lifestyle and financially set. What could possibly make either one want to take a chance on getting hurt again? They had hurt each other pretty badly before and had been hurt also by others. Alex kept saying that he was not going to make the same mistakes he made last time.

On Tuesday Laura remembered to check with Jayne about how she managed to talk with Alex about her in the first place. It was a real shock to learn from Jayne that her father had been buried on Sunday. "What?! Why didn't you let me know?"

"I've been so crazy, Laura, I didn't talk to anyone."

"Would it be okay if I came by?"

"It would be great. Bring Alex too."

Laura and Alex made plans to go by Jayne's. Laura stopped by Wal-Mart on the way home to find something to wear. Being that she had not dated in eighteen years there was quite a strain on her wardrobe. She thought, going in, "I need something dark, casual, fat covering, with some kind of appeal." Wal-Mart came through. She found a plain navy blue knit stirrups pant set with a long top. She was set. The night went as well as could be expected with Jayne in such a sad mess.

# The Wreck

Wednesday morning was beautiful. It was amazing that the weather was holding so well. Normally, by this time in September things were really cooling down. These highs in the low eighties could last forever as far as Laura was concerned. Dylan was in the shower and David was ironing a shirt for school. When he came out of the utility room he said, "Mom, there's something we need to add to our list for home improvements." Laura held her breath waiting to hear of a new crisis. Then David added, "We need a new ironing board. That thing is the pits."

"Okay, we'll put it on the list."

David finished ironing his favorite shirt, a blue and white striped, and finished dressing. He bid his farewells, "Have a good day!"

"Thanks, Hon. You have a good day, too, and please be careful."

"I will. Tell Dylan to walk up to the corner, if he can. Later." And he was gone. David had not spent his two years working for nothing. He had saved his money for his car, actually found it on the Internet, and had made every payment for almost a year. He bought the car before he was sixteen and used it to learn to drive, so he was no stranger to it when he got his license. David had recently talked his Mom into some new wheels, but he was paying for them too. Part of his responsibility for all his privileges was to pick up his little brother after school. He had just enough time to do this before going to work. Only a mother could imagine how much Laura loved these boys and how proud she was of them.

Laura looked at the new navy blue outfit still out from last night and thought, "Why not? At least she would be comfortable." And on it went. She gathered her things, dropped Dylan off at school and headed for the Technology Center. It promised to be a good day; it was Bob's fiftieth birthday. Everyone was bringing food and gifts. Laura had meatballs and a picture taken of Bob resting on a case of wine and pretending to be a street bum in Seattle. The beard worked, but the jacket and new tennis shoes gave him away.

At lunch it was decided to take the phones off the hook for the fifteen minutes it would take to eat lunch. If everyone ate in shifts, someone would be finished to answer the phone after that much time. Lunch was wonderful. Bob had just opened Laura's present when there was a loud knock at the door. Laura was the closest so she went. Betty from the next office stood there breathless. "Laura, David has been in a terrible wreck. You must come take this phone call."

How do you think and what do you feel when your life stops in front of you? As she walked down the steps and across the parking lot, Laura prayed her silent prayer. Her feet felt like lead and she was sure she would never get to the next building. Someone came out of Betty's building and yelled, "It's not David. It's not David. Go on back."

Laura turned around and entered her own office building. People around the table were just beginning to notice something odd. Laura went straight to the phone, thinking, "Okay, David, if its not you, where are you?" She frantically dialed his beeper with their 911 signal, hoping for a quick reply. Betty came running in the door. "It is David. Come on." And they were off again.

Lisa from the high school was on the line. "Laura, David has been in a very bad wreck. He is being airlifted to Carolinas Medical. You need to go there at once."

"Someone just said it wasn't David. Are you sure?"

"I am very sure. I wish it wasn't David, but it is. Go to the hospital."

"Should I come to the wreck?"

"No, everything will be taken care of here. Go to the hospital. And, Laura, you need to hurry."

Laura walked back into her office and to her desk. The shock was descending as she picked up pocketbook and keys. Jennifer came to her office door and said, "What is going on here. Did someone say something about a wreck?'

"Yes, David has been in a wreck and he is being airlifted to Carolinas Medical. I'm supposed to go there right now." Laura headed for the door.

Jennifer responded quickly, "Get in my car. I will drive you."

Laura walked to Vonda's desk. "Vonda, David has been in a wreck. Please call John over at Caldwell Middle, ask him to find Dylan and take care of him. I don't want any high school kids getting to Dylan before an adult does. David was supposed to pick him up."

"We'll take care of Dylan. Go on," was the reply.

They left straight away. Laura clutched her telephone. They prayed. They called the hospital for directions and called Vonda to check in. John had Dylan and was headed for the hospital with him. Dianne had called Laura at the office just as Vonda was trying to find her number. Dianne was calling relatives in Charlotte so someone would come to the hospital. The minutes were hours. The thirty-minute trip seemed to take days. Laura called Alex.

"Hello"

"Alex, I've got some bad news. David has been in a wreck and he is being air lifted to Carolinas Medical."

"Do you know about his injuries?"

"I don't even know if he is alive."

"Do you want me to come?"

"Yes, come to the emergency room. Look for the trauma unit signs."

"I'm on my way."

There were not many people in the waiting room. It was in two sections divided by chairs and tables and lamps. There was no one Laura recognized. Laura went to the desk. "I'm Laura McDowell. My son, David, was in a wreck and has been airlifted in. Do you know of his condition or if I might see him?"

"I'll let them know you are here. Are you alone?" Laura nodded her head. "Then please have a seat and someone will be out to talk to you. David should be in the emergency room on the other side of those glass doors."

Unable to sit, Laura stood, and stared through the glass doors, hoping and praying to get a glimpse of David and for David to be all right and knowing that she was there. Several people who were sitting close to the desk moved to the back of the waiting area. A lady came through the glass doors and approached Laura. "Are you David's parent?"

"Yes. How is he?"

"The doctor will be out to speak with you, but I need to get you to sign a 'consent for treatment form'."

"Of course, anything you need."

"When they put David in the helicopter he did not have any identification on him. His shirt is available, if you would look at it. It would be very helpful to have positive identification."

"Sure." Laura held her breath while the lady fetched the shirt. 'Maybe it won't be David's. Maybe it wasn't him after all. What was he wearing this morning?' were the thoughts going through this poor woman's head. After what seemed like the second eternity, the lady returned carrying a piece of material that was obviously not David's shirt. With a heart as heavy as lead, Laura identified the swatch. "It's not David's shirt, it's his underwear." The forms got signed. Laura sat down.

Jennifer came in from parking the car. Uncle Don and Aunt Helen came in. Dylan and John arrived. Laura tried to explain everything she did not know to Dylan. Alex came in. Laura introduced him to everyone. She said to Dylan, "I'm sorry you had to meet under these circumstances, but I needed for Alex to be here."

Jim Wilkins came from the emergency room and introduced himself. "I am a chaplain here at the hospital. I have just come from David's room. We could have a prayer, if you wish." Jim's voice encompassed the entire room. It was a beautiful, bold prayer, leaving no doubt what was desired for David.

Sue and Lisa, Assistant Principals from Caldwell High came in. Laura was very concerned about how the wreck happened and if there were other parents in her situation and if David had been at fault. Sue relayed the story. "No, it was not David's fault. David was taking Ryan to find his car after school. It seems that Steven had taken Ryan's car when he had been asked to leave school for cutting a class. Steven had not returned the car so David and Ryan were going to find it. About a half-mile from the school they were struck head on by Steven who was driving Ryan's car very fast on the wrong side of the road. The other children were taken to a closer hospital. None of their injuries appeared to be serious."

Laura felt a major relief in the midst of her heartbreak. At least the others were safe and David was not at fault. Joan Coley, the Assistant Superintendent, came in. She confirmed the story and had word that the other boys were fine. She also had news that David's car had been towed and that Channel Eight had been around filming and was planning to air the wreck on the five o'clock news. Laura borrowed Alex's phone and went outside to call Channel Eight.

"May I speak to someone in the news room please?"

"Hello."

"This is Laura McDowell. I understand your news crew has been at Caldwell High School this afternoon filming a wreck."

"Yes, that is correct."

"I also understand that you are planning to air this on the 5 o'clock news."

"Yes, that is correct, too."

"Well, my son was the one airlifted to the hospital and I really don't need this on the news so quickly."

"We are in the news business and people have the right to know."

"Okay, listen to me for a minute. I have elderly relatives in the Charlotte area that watch your news every evening. I'm afraid that if they see David's car and hear his name that they could have heart attacks. Four of them are over 89 years old. They watch your station because my father worked there for thirty years."

"Well, you know, it's still the news. What did your father do here at Channel Eight?"

"My father was chief engineer for 30 years. He passed away about a year after your new building was built. The flags out front and the memorial are dedicated to him. In fact, I worked there for six years myself. So, if you have trouble making a decision here, please remember that David is a minor and I do not want his name released. If that doesn't do it, then go outside, take a long look at those flags and see if your conscience won't permit you to make the right decision."

"Thank you. I hope David will be all right."

"Thank you. I have not seen him yet. I don't know of his injuries. I think he is still alive and I guess I need to get back to the waiting room. Goodbye." Laura called Dianne to let her know what was happening. She was still notifying people and making plans to come.

Some of David's closest friends from school began arriving.

Eventually a doctor appeared from the emergency room. He located Laura and sat down beside her. "I have done what I could do for your son's leg. It is in very bad shape and I'm almost sure he will lose it. It has been shattered below the knee. His leg, however, is not his most serious injury. He has a massive blood clot in his brain from his head injury. He did not hit his head and there are no external marks on his head or face, but the injury occurred from the impact of the car stopping so abruptly.

He will be going on to neurosurgery immediately and you will need to move upstairs to that waiting room. When Dr. Henry is finished, he will come out and talk to you. David also has a broken femur in his left leg and a compound fracture to his left arm. We do not know of anything else at this time, but as we are dealing with the most serious injuries first, the x-rays and scans will continue. If there is anyone else you should call, you should do so pretty soon. Someone will be down in a minute to take you to the surgery waiting room." And he shook hands and left.

Laura asked Jim for another prayer. As he finished, they noticed a stretcher moving on the other side of the door. Laura thought, 'There goes my son. God, please be with him'.

The upstairs waiting room was much larger. There were several phones and a manned reception desk. The phones rang off the hook. People answered questions as best they could. Alex and Laura exchanged distant worried glances. Dylan was holding up okay, but everyone seemed to be on another planet or something. As Laura was heading across the room to answer a phone call, the car showed up on the news. It was at that instant that Laura knew the meaning of the expression, 'Stopped dead in your tracks.' You could not even tell that the piece of metal was a car. You could see a deflated air bag and part of the windshield on what should have been the front seat. The car had no front or side or top. No front wheel. The reporter was remarking about teenage drivers. No names were mentioned. How the child was still alive was a mystery.

It was time to call Jeff. Laura found a private room and with Dylan at her side dialed the number.

"Hello" came the voice through the phone.

"Hi, Jeff, this is Laura"

"Hey, how are you?"

"Well, I've been better. I have some bad news. Are you sitting down? If not, sit down and listen real good."

"Oh my God, it's one of the boys, isn't it?"

"Yes, now listen up. David was in a wreck this afternoon leaving school. It was not his fault. Another student hit him. He has just gone into surgery. You need to pack a bag and come to Carolinas Medical Center, the surgery waiting room on the fifth floor. You remember the hospital, you had some treatments here?"

"Yes, I remember."

"Okay. Hurry, but do not be careless. David will need us both. It is very serious."

"Laura, is he going to die?"

"I don't know. He was hit head on. He has a neurosurgeon with him now. He has two broken legs and a broken arm. His right leg is very severe. Please be careful."

"Okay. I'm on my way."

"See you soon."

More and more people were entering the waiting room. The entire Wednesday night prayer group was there except Wesley and Sally. They were baby-sitting for Ben and Margaret. Di came. Cindy Edwards came, went back home, keyed off Laura's alarm, got Walker's number, and then called back so Laura could get in touch with him. Alex left so as not to be a bother or cause any stress when Jeff arrived. Laura had strict orders to call him. Daniel, Catherine, and Walter, three of Laura's cousins came. David's girlfriend, Beverly, and her father arrived. It was sit and wait time. Some people ate supper. Laura drank some coffee. The phones were ringing off the hook. Laura spoke to Daniel about the wreck. He was an attorney and just happened to specialize in accidents. He was down to earth and nice, not like some lawyers, and Laura told him to please handle whatever needed to be done. Everyone was still trying to piece together what happened. It seemed so strange that the car belonging to his passenger had hit David.

The helicopter pilot came by to see Laura when he got off duty. He said that David had been talking to him on the way to the hospital. He had eventually passed out, probably from pain, but he had a good feeling about David's recovery. He just wanted Laura to know and to say he would be praying for David.

Laura was getting calls from all over about people praying for David. There was a meeting of three hundred or so youth at one church and they were praying. David was going onto prayer chains in Indonesia and India. Prayer requests were going out on the Internet. Everyone was praying for David. Jim had more prayers. Ben had prayers.

David made the late evening news too. Jeff arrived. Some of Laura's closest kin were not on the best of terms with him, but who can you fault when a child's life is at stake?

It was well after midnight when the doctors arrived from the surgery. A small, tight knit group gathered in the hall. Dr. Henry spoke first. "David had a large blood clot on the right side of his brain. There were no external wounds to the head so the blood clot occurred from the impact of the brain moving forward and stopping abruptly. We were able to remove the clot, cleanly and thoroughly. Now we will wait and see. He has a very severe injury and we can not say that he is completely out of the woods."

"Doctor, is there brain damage?" came the question from Jeff.

"Well, of course, there is brain damage. How much and how severe, we will have to wait and see," replied Dr. Henry, and harshly.

Dr. Wittenberg spoke next. "David's left arm suffered a compound fracture. We have set his arm and put in a plate. It is fixed and healing. His left leg suffered a break in the femur. Due to the time allowed by 'neuro' we did not set his leg, we inserted a fixator to keep it immobile and when the time is right, we will set his left leg. His right leg was shattered, both bones, below the knee. We have also done what time would allow with that leg. It also has a fixator. The leg still has an open wound that will require plastic surgery as soon as possible. We will have to wait on neuro to release David to us before we can do any more surgery." Then he added looking straight into Laura's eyes, "I know you were told in emergency that David would lose his right leg. There are many things that you can do with bones to keep this from happening. There will be plastic surgery. There can be bone graphs. His leg is pretty badly damaged, but I do think he has a good chance to keep it."

Laura stood in front of the doctors tired, stunned, and eternally grateful. She said, "Thank you."

Dr. Henry replied, "David is in recovery. He will be moved to his room in trauma in a little while. You need to move to the Trauma ICU waiting room down the hall. They will call for you there when you can see him."

At this point lots of people took their leave. Some stayed to get a look at David. Some journeyed to the cafeteria for a snack. Jeff and Dylan headed to the cafeteria. Laura headed to the phone.

The Trauma ICU waiting room was smaller and there was no coffee. There were other families already there; people with loved ones in better or worse shape than David. It was hard to tell, but for sure there were several lives hanging in the balance. People were beginning to put sleeping bags on the floor for another long night of waiting. Laura couldn't even sit down. In an hour or two they called for David's family. He could be seen now.

Laura, Dylan, Jeff, Catherine, Di, Jim, and other remainees entered the two double doors and the private room on the right. They were instructed to wash their hands before approaching the bed. There he was, the near-angel of her heart, the co-owner of her happiness, her pride and joy. How could this be? How could her beautiful, perfect son be in this condition? Look at him. He was so peaceful and still, just like he was sleeping. There was a slight mark on his face from the airbag. There were major staples from the surgery, with a probe and a draining tube coming from his head. His head was shaved on one side from the surgery. His beautiful long eyelashes rested on his face. His left arm was in a bandage. There was a major metal contraption in his left thigh and in his right calf. You could see a bandaged spot on his right leg. That must be where the tissue was missing and the plastic surgery will be. His mother could just look at all this equipment. There were six computers attached to various parts of his body. He had a respirator tube coming from his mouth leading to a large machine and then to a computer. It was supplying David with oxygen and measuring the amount of pure oxygen he was receiving. It also measured how much, if any, David was breathing on his own. There was an ET like attachment, or so it was nicknamed by Dylan due to the little red light, to one of his fingers to measure the amount of oxygen actually reaching his brain. All of these computers fed into a monitor on the wall so a read out of all statistics could be seen at once. The nurse explained that although David was in a coma prior to the surgery, he had also been placed in a chemically induced coma to reduce brain activity and to give his brain a chance to rest. He was also chemically paralyzed for the same reason. There needed to be as little noise and disturbance as possible. The next 48 hours were very critical. Laura asked if she could touch her son. Yes, was the answer, and the best place would probably be the right hand. That was the only limb that had no injuries. Laura touched his hand, told David how much she loved him, and asked him to fight hard, and try to get well. She said, "Angel, I know you are tired, but try real hard. You know that we will be here with you and that we love you."

Everyone held hands, including the nurse, around David, and Jim prayed to the Lord, "Almighty God, the Greatest Physician, we ask to save David. We pray to Your Word, Lord. You said; Ask and it shall be done. We ask you to save David and send him back to us 100%. We ask you to be with this family and these friends and give them the strength they need and the comfort they need. Let them know that You, Lord, are with them and with David during their hour of need. We praise Your Name, Lord, and give to You all the praise and glory for the healing of your child, David. In the name of Your Holy Son, we pray and ask these things of You. Amen."

Laura was sure that the Lord had heard the prayer from Jim. It was so booming and bold and wonderful. It was such a reassurance to have Jim around. She really did not understand all the hospital workings yet, but she felt secure. David began to shake and tremble. "What is that?"

The nurse replied, "That is just a reaction to the trauma. I have let the doctor know and he will give him something for it shortly."

Laura asked, "Is David in pain?"

"No," the nurse replied, "He is being given morphine along with the coma inducing and paralysis inducing drug. If he were in pain, we would be able to tell it from the vital signs on the computer screen."

"He looks like an angel, doesn't he?"

"Yes, I can tell he is a fine young man."

The nurse soon told the family that they needed to return to the waiting room. It was time for meds and some work on David. She assured Laura that she would send for her if there were any changes in David's condition. Laura kissed David, held his hand; told him she loved him and would be nearby. She left for the waiting room.

It would be mid-morning before Dianne arrived. Catherine and Di chose to stay the night with Laura. Catherine did not work and Daniel, Di's (Buffett concert) husband would teach class for her tomorrow. Dylan and Jeff made pallets on the floor while the women took a turn at what had to be the most uncomfortable chairs in the world. A hospital employee handed everyone a blanket. It was impossible to get comfortable. The chair backs were low, and short of seat space. On top of that, they were attached at the arms so if you moved one, you had to move two or three. Laura sat with the blanket around her and tried to figure out how it got to be 5AM. Sleep was not going to happen. She could alternate between silent tears and silent prayers.

At seven everyone in the waiting room was abruptly awakened by an attendant explaining that the cleaning crew had arrived. Everyone needed to turn in their blankets and vacate the room for cleaning. The room had to be thoroughly cleaned, and please do not talk to or disturb the cleaning crew for they must concentrate on what they were doing. The room must be sanitized because people left from here to visit ICU and the germs carried with them must be minimized.

Jeff and Dylan took some things to the car. Laura, Catherine, and Di went to the cafeteria for breakfast. Catherine said she would stay with Laura until Dianne arrived. Laura choked down some grits and tried a cup of coffee. 'What's to do from here?' she thought, 'I have three dollars, no toothbrush, and no idea of what I am doing. I guess there is a gift shop somewhere. I have my little credit card. Lord, I am lost. I can't focus, much less think. Where is Dylan? I need to keep him safe.'

When they arrived back at the waiting room, the phones were ringing off the hooks. The first call Laura took was from Jayne. "How are things this morning?" was the question. For some reason it took Laura by surprise. She replied, "Well, we have a morning. We made it through the night. We have a morning. We can thank the Lord for that."

The schools, church, office, friends, all called. The injuries were explained in detail. Prayers were requested on David's behalf. No, Laura did not need anything. She was fine. No, there was no more immediate surgery planned for David.

The 9:30 visit found David to be very much the same. The machines were starting to make a little more sense. Some of David's friends showed up for the visit. Beverly said there was no way she could be in school because she was too upset. Beverly also said that she and David were supposed to meet at three, but he did not show up, so she went on home. Jackson called and said David had been in a wreck. She thought he was kidding. After a couple more phone calls, she knew it was true and knew she had to get to the hospital. She was sorry she did not get there until nine last night. Beverly stayed the rest of the day and helped man the phones.

The police were waiting for Laura in the hall. They explained how the accident occurred, who had been treated and released at the other hospital. No, they had not filed any charges, as of yet. They were waiting to see how David would do. In other words, if David did not make it, the charges would be different, and they only wanted to file once. Laura expressed her concern about revengeful acts against Steven. She asked the officers to please speak out at any student gathering and express her concern. We don't need anyone else hurt. We need for everyone to pray and be positive.

Dianne arrived around twelve. She brought a sleeping bag. She made Laura go wash her face and clean up some, and supplied her with some deodorant. Alex delivered a toothbrush and toothpaste to the front door for Laura. He did not come in because he absolutely did not want to cause any more hardship for Jeff.

Visiting the trauma unit only occurred at 9:30AM, 1:30PM, 4:30PM, and 8:30PM. Sometimes this could not occur. If a patient was having special treatment or serious attention was required, all visitors waited in the hall. Sometimes visiting was postponed for hours or even canceled. This was all for the good of the patients, so everybody understood. Laura was beginning to understand just how long she could go without sitting down. At this point, any physical strain was minor compared to the reward of seeing David. Just to watch him was worth more than anything else was in this world. She was so glad to have an opportunity to see him. After seeing the car on TV, she did not think she would ever have the chance to see her precious David again.

Months later Laura would learn that she was certainly not alone in this. The police on the scene did not think David would make it to the hospital. He stopped breathing. The rescue squad had to use the "Jaws of Life" on both sides of his car to get him out. The impact that broke both his legs also sent his legs to the passenger side of the car. They had to remove the pedals from his right leg. They believed that if he lived, he would live without legs. The first officer on the scene was also the mother of a Caldwell High School student. She went by Laura's office after the wreck. Her words to the secretary were, "Miracles happen everyday, but it is going to take a super miracle for David to pull through this."

As Thursday moved along the nurse explained as much as possible to Laura. "The internal cranial pressure (ICP) is a little higher than we would like it. Normally, this pressure hovers around zero with 15 being the highest we like to see. A high pressure can cause more brain damage and allow infection to set in. David's, as you can see, is hovering around 20. We will report this to the doctor and probably give him some additional mannitol. That's what he is being given for swelling. This hospital is one of a few that really tries to treat head injuries. Most of them operate on just wait and see."

"Yes, we are lucky to live so close to this trauma center. It only took eight minutes by air to get him here," Laura replied as her eyes became glued to the ICP readout on the monitor. Soon she located the ICP machine, which published the readout, a fraction of a second before the monitor. For the next 48 hours her eyes would focus next to nowhere else.

It seemed like hundreds of people came and went. Actually, it was more than sixty and Laura knew she would never keep track of it. So many of David's friends and teachers came. At every chance, Laura urged them to be positive and pray. Please do not take anything out on the others involved in the wreck. Barry Yount, the psychologist David had seen years earlier over the anxiety problem, came. People from Laura's office and people she had worked with at some previous time came. Old friends came. It was the greatest diversion ever. Her cousin, Daniel, called to say that the Little family had filed a claim against her insurance since Ryan was a passenger in David's car. This news made visits by the Little family very difficult, but they were tolerated and treated respectfully. Laura's bridge club, made up of middle school teachers, came and brought a school board member with them. Patty said, "We knew that we could not play bridge while we were worried about David, so we came here. We brought you a few things." A few of them went into the 8:30 visit, most waited outside. David's ICP's were not better. In fact, now they were around 24 or 25. The nurse expressed concern. She also said that David was given additional medication and doubted that he could have more. Laura was feeling uneasy, at best. There were more prayers for the miracle.

When Laura returned to the waiting room, it was approaching ten o'clock. It appeared to be Dylan and Dianne for the night. Jeff had missed all the visits all day. He had gone to look at the car, talk to people, and maybe go home for something. Laura suspected medication. He had called around six to say he would be there soon. He did not even ask about David. Nothing had changed with this man. He absolutely could not focus on anything but what he wanted. Dylan had eaten with Dianne when the bridge club came. Laura did not eat. In fact, she had not eaten since breakfast. When she looked through the bridge club stuff, she found all sorts of goodies. When she looked in the envelope, she found three hundred dollars.

Jeff returned with tales of wrecked cars, police, attorneys, etc. He and Dylan prepared for their second night on the floor. Dianne and Laura stretched out too. As uncomfortable as it was, with lights shining directly in your face, there were no light switches; it was still better than trying to sleep in one of those chairs. By morning Jeff was gone again.

After the 7AM-wakeup call and breakfast, Laura, Dianne, and Dylan returned to the waiting room to take calls and wait for the 9:30 visit. Jeff appeared. It seems that he sneaked into David's room to see him since he missed the visits yesterday. He was full of bad news. It seemed that David's ICP's had climbed to 67 early this morning.

Laura made great haste to ICU. Luckily, they allowed her to come in ahead of schedule, too. The nurse confirmed Jeff's story. No, it did not look good. The highest she had ever seen ICP's, and the patient live, was 80, and that caused severe brain damage. One thing Laura noticed was that you were told things on a need to know basis, unless you asked the right question. The nurse had contacted Dr. Henry but he was in surgery.

He would be up to talk to the family as soon as he could. For right now, everything that could be done for David was being done. It was best now to wait and to pray.

Laura stood motionless taking in the situation and watching her beautiful son. She glanced at the ICP machine and noticed the numbers start to climb, 24, 25, 26, 28, 30, and she tried to say, "They are climbing again." By the time she got out the sentence they were at 45 and by the time the nurse got her hands on Laura's shoulders to turn her towards the door, they were on 58 and still going.

For the first time since the wreck, the clouds cleared and Laura knew her son was going to die. She could hardly make it to the waiting room, where she relayed the horror to Dylan and Dianne. They called her pastor, work, David's school, Dylan's school, and two family members asking for prayers. He was so sick. Christy, a church family member, came in. She held Laura's hands and prayed for David. Tears streamed down Laura's face for she was beyond desperation.

In an hour or so the family was called back to one of the smaller waiting rooms for a conference with Dr. Henry. It was one of those dreaded waiting rooms where no one wants to be. It was one of those rooms where you hear terrible things about a family member. Dylan sat on the chair with Laura. She held onto him tightly. Jeff came in just as Dr. Henry began to speak. "David, as I'm sure you know, is very, very, sick. His condition at this moment is critical and there is not much that can be done to help him. What I can do is to insert another drainage tube. The problem is that there is intense swelling. There is not much liquid, if any, left around the brain to drain. I have never seen this amount of swelling from this type of head injury. We can try this procedure and see if we get any results, but I do not want to get your hopes up. We are not dealing with large amounts of fluid; we are dealing with swollen tissue that cannot drain. Do you understand what I am telling you about the condition of David?"

Laura nodded.

The doctor continued just to make sure, "I lose patients in this condition. I lose young ones and old ones. I want you to be prepared for whichever way this goes. Do you understand?"

Laura nodded.

"Okay, I just want you to be prepared."

"Will you take David to surgery?"

"No, we will do the procedure in ICU."

"When?"

"As soon as I leave this room."

"If you think of anything else you can do, even if it is not tried and true, please do it."

Jeff continued to ask some questions. When he began talking about his own surgeries, Laura interrupted, "Excuse me, but I think we need to stop talking. Dr. Henry has a very important procedure to perform, and I think we need to let him go do it."

"You're right. All of this can wait," replied Jeff.

Dr. Henry took his exit. The family sat in shock. In a few minutes Jeff went out. While Dianne went for a smoke, Laura remained in the little room. She noticed the phone beside her but did not use it. Someone took Dylan to lunch. Laura waited for news. She waited for the 1:30 visit. For her son to die. For him to live. For the first time she envisioned a funeral, but she kept seeing David standing alive by an empty casket. She prayed to the Lord to save her son. She called Alex. When Dianne returned, Laura said, "What do I do now? Do I start thinking about a funeral?"

Dianne said in her best big sister voice, "No, now you just get those thoughts out of your head. David is going to be fine. He has more to fight with than most people do or he wouldn't be here now. Do not give up on him. We can not allow anything but positive thoughts to be in this room or around him, so you just think about something else."

Laura began to think about all the things David had to fight with. He was strong. He was in an adult body that was fine-tuned due to his bicycle competition. His body had suffered very little abuse, apart from an occasional cigarette and one or two joints (before he got caught by Mama). His drug tests afterwards had never produced any positive results. He had experienced sex, was strong willed and determined. It showed in the biking feats that he was able to accomplish. David was willing to try hard and work for what he wanted. He had experienced just enough of an adult life, not to leave him scared, but to inspire him to want more. David was a Christian but he would not want to leave Laura and Dylan to take care of themselves. If anyone could make it, he could. So there. 'Let's continue to pray and hope for the miracle,' she thought.

The minutes passed. A few hours passed. Jennifer came. Joan came. Vonda and Robin left their convention in Greenville and drove to the hospital for Robin to pray for David. It was a beautiful prayer. It seemed like hundreds of people came to see David. When the last visit was over, Laura decided to try to sleep on the love seat in the little room. The nurses promised to come for her if there was a change in David. As of now, the ICP's were still in the low twenties, but there had been no more hideous spiking. Her sleep was disturbed at best. All night long she prayed. More than once she would dose off before she added, "In Jesus' name I pray." In her tormented sleep she feared her prayers were not getting through. Around five, she began her prayers with "Dear Heavenly Father, through Jesus Christ, I pray." At daybreak she ventured to the chapel for a private talk with the Lord.

There was another morning. When Laura went into visit, the ICP's were down to 15. The indicator flashed "15, 14, 15, 13, 14, 15, 13, 12, 14, 15." By afternoon they were flashing "12, 11, 10, 13, 12." Dianne and Laura noticed that if there was complete silence, the ICP's hovered around eleven. When they talked, they rose to 13 and 14. This was some strong evidence that David could hear his Mom's voice and probably thought he had two moms since Dianne and Laura sounded exactly alike or at least sense her presence. By evening, the readings were around ten with some being single digits. The miracle was in progress. The angels were present. You could feel it in the room.

From 4PM to 10PM on Saturday David had more than forty visitors. Laura made some calls requesting no visitors on Sunday. She needed some time alone with her sons and felt that Sunday needed to be the day.

When Laura entered the ICU the nurse was grinning. She said, "Look at the ICP's." The display read, "4". As Laura watched, she saw it go to zero. Praise the Lord. What a beautiful day! Laura spent some time watching David and then went to the Chapel to say her "Thank you." Jeff questioned the nurse about his concern for the ICP's being too low. He was assured that they were not.

Before the next 1:30 visit Laura felt confident enough to go to the cafeteria for lunch. She went alone. Everyone else had eaten. Dylan came down in the middle of her meal to report that David had overridden the ventilator and broken through the chemically induced paralysis and began breathing on his own. This had caused his ICP's to go up to 47. They did not know why this had happened and the doctors were all upset. They were going to put him under deeper. There was no need in hurrying back upstairs because they would not let her in the room if they were working and it was a known fact that she had no ability to help. All she could do was pray. She certainly could not finish her lunch so she kept company with Dylan, her motivation. What a support and strong young man he had been. He held his brother's hand, laughed and cried with the adults. How many thirteen-year-olds could do this for this long without one thought for themselves?

The 1:30 visit was allowed and extremely calm. The ICP's were down again. David showed no signs of stress. His breathing was fine. This was so strange. What had caused David to push himself so? How could he possibly be strong enough to override the ventilator? How could he muster the strength to override the paralysis to then override the ventilator? What a fighter! But what was going on? What did David know or sense about his condition? Was anyone making an effort to find out? Laura was glad to have just a few visitors today.

She spent the remainder of the afternoon in the little room outside ICU. Dianne and Dylan kept her company. Jeff and visitors wandered in and out. She talked to Alex a few times. They went through all the goodies from bridge club. Dylan made tea for everyone. Jim came by and went in to check on David. He reported no change. At one point Laura heard the major alarm sound in ICU and noticed people scurrying about. No one sent for her so she rested easy. Later she learned, when she was asked for another consent, what had happened to David and why he started his own breathing. During the afternoon they attempted to check the placement of David's feeding tube. In doing so, they managed to dislodge his respirator tube leading to his lungs. This is what caused all the alarms and scurrying people that Laura had observed. David was without breath for a few minutes as they reinserted the tube. Scary. David had been able to breath on his own at twelve, but at three he was too far under to be of any help. When they reinserted the tube and ran some tests they noticed that David was not getting as much air from his right lung as from his left lung. There it was. That was it. He had aspirated some object in the wreck and it was just now creating enough havoc in his lung for it to register on a machine. David, however, sensed this four hours ago and tried to give himself more oxygen. He breathed on his own. Don't try to tell Laura that her son wasn't a fighter. What a kid! The respiratory people were amazed. The ICP people were concerned. At this point, Laura had to give her consent for a Bronchoscopy. This was a procedure to clean out David's lung and retrieve whatever was causing the commotion. They would send it to the lab for tests and see if it would grow a culture. Yes, it would be done in the room right after the visiting.

Laura sat in the waiting room by herself. She looked up to see two young men and their parents. The father introduced himself as Bill Lawrence, and his wife and sons. When it hit Laura that in front of her sat Steven Lawrence, the child driving the other car, an unbelievable calm descended through her entire body. She had talked to kids since Wednesday about Steven and staying positive. Now it was her turn. Bill said, "Mrs. McDowell, Steven has something he would like to say to you."

"Okay, Steven, go ahead."

"Mrs. McDowell, I am really sorry about what I have done. I always liked David and I would never do anything to harm him. I wish I could trade places with him."

"Steven, I know that you would never start a car, run it up to seventy miles per hour and purposely run it into David. No one would do that. This was an accident. It could have been avoided, but it was not done on purpose. Now, about trading places with David, I know that you really would not want to do that. I appreciate your coming here, I know that took a lot of nerve and I admire you for it, but I don't think you would really like to trade places with David."

"Yes, I would." And the room fell silent.

Laura added to Steven's mother, "I have spoken to David's friends about being positive and being nice to Steven. I understand that he is returning to school on Monday. I don't want any confrontations and have told them so. We need to keep things positive and to pray for David."

"Thank you."

"I also spoke to Dylan's friends at the Middle School because I don't want anything unpleasant to be said to your younger one."

Her mouth fell open and Steven's mother replied, "I had not even thought of that. You are very kind. Thank you."

Steven asked if he could see David. It was okay with Laura, if ICU would let him in. They did. They understood the special circumstances. David had a new machine. This one included a TV monitor that showed the inside of David's right lung. Steven stood in awe of David's condition and all the machines. He cried. His dad stood speechless. Laura had suggested that the younger child wait with his mom. She was thankful of that decision now. She had been watching David for what seemed to be an eternity and was completely used to the all the tubes and machines. It would be a shock to anyone else.

No sooner had the Lawrence's left than the room filled with more visitors. Jeff passed the Lawrence's on the way out, but did not figure it out until they had already passed. Laura was more than thankful that Jeff had not been present. He would surely have made a terrible scene and made matters worse. The kids were talking about Steven being there. Laura said, "Now, listen up. What I want you to do is drive carefully. I don't want anyone driving crazy because you are mad. The last thing we need is for someone else getting hurt. I want you folks to stay positive so David can feel the energy. I want you to pray for David and I want you to drive carefully. If all of this does not keep you positive and give you enough to do, then I want you to come see me and I will give you a list of things to do."

Everyone was calming down a little when Sarah entered the room. Now, Sarah was not very popular with some of David's best friends. She was David's ex-girl and responsible for some of his worst habits and adult experiences. She was actually a very sweet girl and her mother had been a prayer warrior for David. Many of his friends left the room. The ones who did not know her remained, including Beverly. She handed Laura a stuffed animal for David and sat down. Wow. What now? What next? Jackson stuck his head in the door. "Where's Jimmy? I thought I saw him?"

Laura replied, "He went downstairs."

Jackson turned to go. Laura excused herself and followed him to the elevator. "Please go back into the room, get Beverly, and take her with you to get something to eat."

"Okay, why?"

"Because that is Sarah sitting in there. Beverly does not know who she is and I don't want to upset Beverly when she realizes what is going on."

"Okay, sure." Jackson went back to retrieve Beverly from a potentially bad situation, leaving Laura and Sarah alone. Laura assured Sarah that her visit was welcomed and appreciated. Yes, she was sure David would want to know she had been there. Yes, please tell your mom that I appreciate her prayers because without a doubt she had been talking to the Lord on David's behalf. Sarah took her leave. Laura decided that it was time to venture about to see where everyone had scattered. For a restful day with her sons, this day was lacking quite a bit.

She ran into Cathy, a former student of Laura's. Now she was a teacher, herself, and a member of the same Bible-study group at the church. Cathy asked, "Did you hear what went on at church this morning?"

"Well, no, no details. Ben called to say they had prayed for David."

"Laura, I have never seen anything like it in my life! I know our church has never done anything like this. Ben told the congregation about David's wreck for the Morning Prayer. When the prayer was finished, Julie Brooks stood and said she felt that the Lord wanted her to pray again for David. The whole service turned into a prayer vigil for David. I mean everyone was up at the altar praying for David. Have you ever seen good Methodists raising their hands above their heads in prayer to the Lord? Well, that's what they were doing! Every one of them! I have never seen anything like it!"

"Do you know what David was doing at 11:30?" and Laura began telling Cathy the story of the breathing, overriding ventilators, paralysis and such. What a happening! There truly is some miracle going on here. Cathy did not stay long. She did not go in to see David. She left to tell the amazing story of David's breathing and why he had the strength to do it.

Laura was looking forward to a peaceful 8:30 visit with her son when David Evens came in with Joe Long. "I know we aren't suppose to visit today, but Joe hasn't seen David yet so we thought we would try."

"It's okay. We will all go in together. Jeff and Dylan are coming too."

It was a pleasant experience until Dr. Slingers came in. He was a doctor assigned to the trauma unit. Jeff asked this fine doctor in front of the visitors and David, "Doctor, what do you think David's chances are?"

"David's chances are not good. I doubt that he will make it." Was his reply and the room fell still. Mouths fell open. Laura looked at Dylan and said, "Dylan, take David and Joe outside while we talk to the doctor." Dr. Slingers looked around and said, "Would you like to discuss this in the hall?" Laura replied, "Yes, I think that would be best, just in case David can hear."

The nurse went with them. The four of them stood in the hallway inside ICU. Laura stood between the doctor and Jeff and faced the nurse. Jeff repeated his question, "What do you think David's chances are?"

"I think David has an excellent chance of not making it." Laura locked eyes with the nurse as the doctor continued. "If he does make it, you will not recognize him. He will certainly not be the person that you have known up till now." Everything after that was pretty much garbled as far as Laura heard. She did not take her eyes off the nurse as she allowed the hurt and pain to soar through her mind and body. She realized that the doctor and Jeff were just babbling on about something. Finally Jeff said, "I don't mean to cut you out of this, Laura, do you have any questions for the doctor?"

"No, I'm still trying to get over his first two statements." With that, Laura turned and walked back into David's room. She stood by her son and cried, cried like a baby as she held his hand and told him she loved him. The nurse came in with a chair for Laura. In a few minutes Dianne came in. The nurse, Laura, and Dianne discussed the situation. There was a wealth of comfort offered, but it wasn't working too well with

Laura. She said, "You know, he did not say anything I have not heard before. I guess it was his manner that has gotten me so. He made it sound so hopeless and it can't be hopeless because David is still here. Where is Dylan?"

Dianne replied, "He's gone with David's friends and Jeff, I think for some supper."

"Well, I just need a few more minutes with David." And as the tears fell silently Laura held David's hand and prayed and cried and prayed and cried. Finally, the nurse said, "It's ten thirty, why don't you take a break for a few minutes? Have you had dinner?"

"No. I'm not sure I had lunch."

"Well, you need to eat. Go get a snack. I promise you I will find you if there is any change in David. I will find you. Go ahead. We will let you back in whenever you want."

And Laura left the ICU unit to return to her little waiting room. Dianne and Dylan looked up. "The nurse told me to take a break. She said I should get some supper, but the cafeteria is closed and I can't think of anything I want. I surely do not want to go anywhere."

"They still have some things left, Dylan and I will get you something. Just rest, we'll be right back." And in the flash of an eye they were gone and Laura was alone, alone with her thoughts and her God.

Fifteen minutes later they were back with some warm soup. Laura had to admit that it tasted pretty good. She was completely crushed. She was without an ounce of energy. She did not have the energy to move out of the chair. She believed that the nurse would come after her. Dylan went to sleep with his Dad. Dianne went out for a smoke and still Laura sat. She felt kneecapped. She was curled up in a little ball.

The phone rang and it was Barry Yount, the psychologist from Caldwell. In his soft-spoken, kind voice, he said, "Laura, I certainly do not make a habit of calling my patients at this late hour. Actually, I don't call them often, at any hour, but I just felt like I needed to check with you.

I was having trouble falling asleep. I had you and David on my mind so much. You know, I keep this little penlight by my bed, just in case there is ever an emergency. Well, I was just thinking about you and David and all of a sudden this little light just came on all by itself. I thought this was a sign to pick up the phone and call. Is everything okay? How is David?"

Laura could not believe her ears. There was no one in the world that would be better to talk to now than Barry Yount. She felt the Lord was watching over her. How could a light come on by itself? Why was Barry thinking of the two of them so? She quickly related the evening's events to Barry, how cruel the doctor had been and how badly it had upset her.

Barry replied, "Laura, I really believe that people who are in comas can hear. Not now, but in the morning, or whenever you feel good enough to go back into David, there is something I want you to tell him. Please tell him that I called. Tell him that I think he is such a fine young man. I have seen him handle such tough situations and deal with things that many people would find overwhelming. I have every hope and trust in him. I know what a fighter he is and I know he will beat this. Please tell him we are praying for him and we know he will be okay."

Laura thanked the good doctor for his kind words and for her own therapy session. "You know, Barry, you have made me feel so much better, I'm going right back to David right now and tell him what you said." And she did.

The nurse smiled as Laura came in. "Are you feeling better?"

"Yes. I've had a real good talk with one of David's doctors. He has some things he wants me to say to David." Laura leaned over to David and shared the words from Dr. Yount. She told the nurse that she just wanted to sit for a while and hold David's hand. This was the day set aside for her to spend some time alone with her son, but she had not really had much time yet. The nurse approved, although the visiting hours were long since passed. Laura sat with David and held is hand, looking at his beautiful face while he rested. She watched all the computers and checked the displays for the correct numbers, trying to absorb the magnitude of the situation. She had wonderful people helping her. She had people watching her house, taking care of animals, and even doing some cleaning. She still had not changed clothes and was bathing in the bathroom sink. Dianne was supplying underwear. Joan brought this wonderful bag with toiletries, snacks, etc. It had really been a lifesaver. Some people had even brought food. There was a chicken pie to die for and baked chicken, grapes, and even pizza. David sure had a lot of people that loved him.

In a little while the nurse told Laura that they needed to work with David. She was welcomed to stay, but she needed to be on the other side of the room for a bit. Laura got up and leaned against the wall. She had full view of David while they checked everything out. After a bit the nurse came up to Laura and inquired, "Laura, are you asleep?"

"Well, I guess I was."

"You might need to have a seat. I'm afraid that you might fall, if you continue to sleep leaning against the wall."

Laura looked at the clock. It was three-thirty in the morning. "I guess what I should do is go on out and come back for visiting. You will call if anything happens?"

The nurse nodded and Laura left for the remainder of the night.

The Monday morning visit was very peaceful. David's ICP's were hovering at zero and his coughing was controlled by cleaning his windpipe. Laura was glad he couldn't feel any of this. When they left ICU, Dianne led Laura to the parking lot. They had been told they needed to move back to the main waiting room. So with arms full of "stuff" they had accumulated they were off to the car. Dianne took the opportunity to have a cigarette and Laura took the opportunity to call Alex. She called him everyday with a report on David along with her office, the church, David's school and Dylan's school. It felt good to be outside. Dianne also announced that they were going to Catherine's after the 1:30 visit to shower and wash their clothes. This was good news because the blue outfit, although less than a week old, seemed to be showing some age. Dianne also told Laura that she did not need to sit in the waiting room between the visits. "I know you are concerned about people coming to visit and your not being there, but it will be better for you to get out some. Maybe Alex can pick you up and take you to supper or go with some of your friends for lunch. They will help you, and it will give you a break from Jeff, too."

"Yes, Ma'am."

It was the best shower and hair-washing Laura ever had. She had already noticed that when she was alone, she could cry. The shower provided the perfect opportunity for that too. She waited in front of the TV in Catherine's bathrobe while her clothes were washed and dried. There was a TV special advertised to be on the six o'clock news about teenage drivers. Every time it was advertised David's car was shown. Sure enough, the wreck was featured in the special. Dylan helped Catherine tape it. Laura watched a Mike Cross special after the news. It was very entertaining and soothing. Supper was delicious. She took a short nap and woke up just in time to dress and head back to the hospital for the 8:30 visit.

The visit was calm and peaceful. David's ICP's were still very low. He was coughing some, but they were keeping his windpipe cleaned. The nurse told Laura that Dr. Henry had ordered a CAT scan for later. This meant that they would be taking David downstairs. Laura told David, "Honey, you are going on a little trip in a while for a test. It won't hurt and it won't take long." Unfortunately, Laura did not mention the trip to Dianne.

When Laura left the ICU she was met by a large group of David's friends waiting to see him. She stopped to greet them and one of them said, "Steven is coming back to school tomorrow." Steven had been spending some quiet time at the suspension center.

Another one said, "He won't be there long."

Laura knew that she had to handle this situation if things were to remain positive. She also knew what Steven would face if she did nothing. She thought for a minute and said, "Is there anyone in this group that has never gone over the speed limit?"

Nobody responded. Then she said, "Do you mean that in this fine group of young people that every one of you has exceeded the speed limit at some time or other?"

There was complete silence and still no response. Laura continued, "Then you are very lucky that no one stepped out in front of your car." Laura paused a minute to gather her thoughts. "I really want things to stay positive for David's sake. I believe it says in the Bible that you need to remove the log from your own eye before you try to remove it from someone else's."

At this point, Dylan, who had just finished Confirmation at the church said, "I believe that is in Luke."

Now that the tension was eased a bit, Laura said, "I know how you feel. I know that this accident did not have to happen, but I want you to focus on David and not on Steven. All I ask is that you pray for David and drive safely. If that is not enough to keep you busy, then come back to me and I'll give you a list of things you can do."

About 10 PM Dianne, Laura, and Dylan were sitting in the little room. They wanted to hold on to it as long as they could, at least until someone else really needed it. Laura heard a noise in the hall, "I'll bet that's David," she said and left the room. Once in the hall she spotted David and two nurses on their way for the CAT scan. "Y'all have a good time, now, and be sure to take care of my boy. Don't forget to mash that tube so David can breathe."

"Okay. We'll be careful!" And they were on the elevator and gone.

Laura was laughing and enjoying her extra minute with David until she turned around to see Dianne, all pale and trembling. "What is going on?

Where are they taking him? Is he okay? He's not having more surgery, is he?!?!"

"Oh, no!" Laura exclaimed, "I forgot to tell you about the CAT scan! He's just going down stairs for a test. He'll be right back. They want make sure there is no new swelling anywhere." Laura was afraid she might have to pick Dianne up off the floor. "I am so sorry. Are you okay?"

"Yes, but I think we need to work on our communication. We never know where Jeff is either."

"Okay, maybe we can do better. Did you see how they were breathing for David?"

"Yes, by hand. I hope they have a machine when they get there. That would be a big responsibility."

"Oh, mercy. I didn't think about it like that." Laura hovered close by until David came back. "Everything okay?"

"Yes. It went well and there is no new swelling. Things are looking pretty good."

It was good to laugh. And another day passed.

On Tuesday morning David was moving his right hand and right leg. Not a lot of movement, but some. It was beyond comprehension that David could move his right leg with it so badly injured. His right hand was understandable, but not his right leg. It still had exposed bone. Laura had to be reassured more than once that David was feeling no pain. He was moving! During the morning visit the nurse was discussing the problems that some patients, in general, encountered in ICU. One of the major concerns was always pneumonia. He said that most of the patients got it at some time or another. In fact, more patients died from pneumonia than anything else. Great, Laura thought, David is sure to have pneumonia after all the lung problems he is having. He was still hooked up to the lung machine. It seemed like each day was taking two steps forward and one step backwards. But, at least, it was going that way rather than one forward and two backwards.

Laura received a phone call from one of David's friends at school. It was David Evens. "Ms. McDowell, we need something more to do to stay positive. We need the list."

Laura was really surprised and she said, "Okay, write this down. Someone needs to take care of Bucky. He needs fresh water and food each day. Someone needs to hose him down with the water hose when it is really hot. He loves it and will play in the water. Let's see, other than that, this would be only if it gets real bad. You know that tree house in the dog lot that you used to play in?"

"Yes, I remember all of that."

"Well, it is just full of ants. It needs to be pulled down and hauled away. I will be glad to pay for any of this. Just get some money from me the next time you are here. Also, there is one other thing. That fence going up the driveway could really use a coat of paint. There is paint for it in the five-gallon bucket in the garage. The color on the bucket is 'Light Moves'. Do you think that's enough?" Laura said laughingly.

"That's a start. I will spread the word. Thanks."

Laura gave David an update and he got off the phone to go back to class.

Among the visitors that morning was a young man named Lance Morris from the Caldwell Times, the hometown paper. He had talked with one of the school superintendents who had gotten permission from Laura to do an article about David. "This is such a community thing. Everyone wants to know what they can do or how they can help. I really appreciate your taking the time to talk with me."

"An article will be fine; in fact, I would really appreciate one, as long as it is done in a positive manner. We don't need to foster any more hostility towards Steven."

"Absolutely."

It was a peaceful day, even with the threat of pneumonia. That evening Laura and Dianne were taking a parking lot break when these thoughts came to Laura and ran right out of her mouth, "You know, I don't know why this happened to David, but I know that the Lord has a plan. I don't know why David was picked to be a part of it, but for some reason, he was. It might be because he is a Christian and the Lord needs to work through him to reach someone else. It might be something in the future that David will do. It might be that he was strong enough to handle this or that his family is strong enough to handle this. You know, you used to ask me if I had any idea of why I was being tested. Now we know why. I needed to be strong enough for this. There have been people praying for David that have never prayed before. Maybe the Lord needed one of them. I don't know and I won't know until I'm dead, but I'll know then, and there has to be a reason, because there is a plan." It was this thought process that got Laura through the turmoil and made her strong. She knew that thousands of people were still praying for David and she knew that the Lord was hearing these prayers. Every chance she got she visited the chapel. It was quiet and peaceful and she could bare her soul. The only difficult part was being alone. It was still very easy to cry when she was alone.

Wednesday brought more changes in David. His movement was becoming more active. You had to be very careful to keep him from throwing off all his covers. He would have died from embarrassment had any of his precious high school friends viewed more of him than showed in his knee length bathing suit. During one of the visits, the doctors approached Laura about consent to do a tracheotomy on David. She was told that he would be much more comfortable with that rather than a tube in his mouth once he started to wake up. It was also to reduce the chance of infection in his lungs because bypassing the mouth would make things more sanitary. Yes, there would be a scar, but it would be small, practically invisible after a while. Of course, Laura agreed to anything for comfort and sanitation. What was happening, that Laura was unaware of, was that little by little, David was being allowed to come to. No one knew what was ahead and what brain functions might be there. Most people were expecting some pretty serious damage.

Laura saw very little of David on Thursday due to the surgery. When she did get to see him late in the afternoon the massive breathing apparatus was gone from his mouth. There was a tube in his throat connected to the ventilator. There was some bleeding but the situation looked better.

The same day the headline of the Caldwell Times read, "Family keeps vigil at comatose son's bedside." It was obvious that Jeff had an input. The article read,

> "David McDowell's parents describe him as one of those kids who was never in trouble or a problem growing up. He was never involved in drugs, didn't swear and his parents can't recall having to spank him.
>
> At Christmas, the McDowell's would choose a needy family in the community and David would sacrifice part of his Christmas to make another family's holiday special.
>
> 'I know parents brag about their kids,' said the 16 year old junior's father, Jeff McDowell, 'but there was always something special about David. He was always thinking about people and considerate of them. People he didn't even know.'
>
> Ironically, the accident that left him in a coma last Wednesday was one of those times.
>
> Shortly after his last class, David and classmate, Ryan Little, pulled out of the Caldwell High School parking lot. They had left to look for Little's car that was being driven by a fellow classmate. They hadn't driven more than a mile when the same car they were looking for crashed head on into them on Barrage Road.
>
> Both of David's legs and his left arm were broken when the front end of his Mitsubishi crumpled on impact. He was pried

from the wreck and airlifted to Carolinas Medical Center in Charlotte.

Since the day of the accident, David's parents and brother have not left the hospital, experiencing what Jeff McDowell refers to as the 'devil's yo-yo.' Every day is filled with ups and downs, hope and despair. Their emotions alternate between anger and joy. David's vital signs fluctuate, as does his condition. At times he breathes on his own or coughs in short gasps, but these times are sporadic and short.

The crash caused a concussion and swelling that has raised the pressure on his brain to life-threatening levels. His legs, which will require numerous operations over the next four years, cannot be set until he is stable and the pressure on his brain has diminished.

On Tuesday, the McDowells' spirits were up. David moved his right arm and leg for the first time since the accident. A good sign for the McDowells, who hang on every change in their son's condition.

'Something as simple as an eyelash twitching could make us jump,' Jeff McDowell said, his voice cracking softly.

David's father looks exhausted and shaken. His eyes are soulful, yet glazed and unfocused as he speaks of his son with admiration.

'I never knew David knew so many people,' he said. 'I never knew we knew so many people.'

Hundreds of students, teachers and friends have come to visit the McDowells over the past week and lend their support. Over the weekend, there were close to 50 people in the room, said Laura McDowell, whose strength and poise have served as inspiration to so many friends and family members.

'I've seen people brought to prayer that may not have prayed before,' she said.

Last Sunday's worship service at Christ United Methodist Church, where the family attends, was turned into a prayer vigil for David.

The McDowells say that they never dreamed they would see so many people coming together the way they have. Friends have given their time to help the family by mowing the lawn, trimming the shrubs, caring for the four animals at the house and painting the McDowell's fence.

A tree house in the back yard had become infested with ants, so David's friends spent two days taking it down and tearing it apart. Now they are waiting to find a trailer to cart it off the property, said Jackson, one of David's close friends.

'(The McDowells') house is like a frat house to us,' Jackson said. 'We were always there, hanging out. He's like our brother.'

Everyone who has come in contact with David sees him as an extraordinary young man. They describe him as honest, dependable, friendly and intelligent.

His social studies teacher, Mary Collins, describes him as the glue to her class. When he's funny, the class is funny. When he's tired, the class is tired.

It's overwhelming to see the many lives David has touched,' Collins said. 'There's not a person in this school that hasn't been hurt by this.'

The Food Lion on Brookview Drive, where David works after school as a bagger, stopped business for 10 minutes the day after the accident for co-workers and customers to offer a silent prayer.

Friends and family remember David in the 24 hours before the accident as being typically David.

Laura McDowell remembers David coming home the evening before the accident. He was never late, she said: he was always home at 9:30.

As usual, David was hungry, and she made him steak and a baked potato. They worked on his math homework together and while she went up to bed, David cleaned and straightened the living room.

The next morning she found David ironing his shirt and getting ready for school.

He had lunch at school with two of his best friends, Jimmy Norris and David Evens, during first lunch before going on to Collins's third period class.

'He was wearing his blue and white striped shirt,' Collins said. 'I always teased him that it made him look like a sailor.'

When the school got word of the accident, Laura McDowell received a call. She rushed to the hospital where she was met by a nurse. The nurse asked her to identify what she called a piece of his shirt.

'The nurse handed me a piece of red plaid cloth. It wasn't his shirt,' she said. 'It was a piece of his boxer shorts. That's how bad the accident was.'

Despite the odds, friends and family are hopeful and remember how David has touched their lives and the difference he has made to so many people.

'I remember my first day of kindergarten,' Evens said. 'I was crying, and David came up to me and said 'Don't cry, my name is David, too.' That's how David is."'

During the evening visit a doctor approached Laura for permission to place a Vena Cava filter in David's artery between his legs and his lungs. This was a small titanium filter designed to stop blood clots from reaching David's lungs. It would only take one blood clot to kill him. Once all the statistics were analyzed there was about a 5% chance of this happening. In fact, it had happened just in the last week to someone in C.I.R our

Rehab. The doctor felt it was especially serious in David's situation due to his right leg being in such dire straits. The major problem was that this was still considered to be experimental. The longest anyone had been with this filter was 20 years. There was no way to remove it as it was attached to a major artery. Only a few trauma centers even considered it. Laura asked the doctor what he would do if this were his son. "I would put it in. No doubt. No questions asked." He said that Laura could think about it and let them know later.

After the visit, Laura went to the chapel to pray. Then she sent word to the doctor to go ahead.

Jeff was gone from the hospital all day.

Friday the filter was inserted. Visits were reduced again. Daniel came by to brief her on the developments and discuss the insurance possibilities and invited her to go out to eat with him and Judy, his wife. It was almost impossible for Laura to make a decision to leave the hospital. Dianne told her she was, in fact, going. She would be back in plenty of time for David's visit. Dylan would go to eat with her and everything would be fine.

It was a wonderful experience. There was an appetizer, steak, potato, salad, and Laura had an Irish coffee to finish it off. It was her first real meal in over a week. She was very nervous and worried to be away from David, but remembering that there was another world outside was good for her. She could hear some of the conversions around her. It seemed that many people were very concerned about things that made no difference whatsoever.

Laura made it back for the 8:30 visit. Dylan had eaten with Dianne and everything was cool. When they went in for the visit the nurse said, "I have something I want you to see." He went to David's right side. He rubbed or lightly poked David's chest and said, "David, David, wake up. Do you hear me? If you hear me, raise your finger. Raise your finger, David."

And David raised his finger.

There was a moment of stunned silence in the room. Then the tears and shouts of joy exploded to the surface. He was in there. David was in there and he was responding to signals! The nurse explained that this was a very good sign. They would ask David to do more over the next few days. Oh what abounding joys! Communication! Praise the Lord.

The nurse was right about the next few days. Every time Laura went in to visit, they were poking at David and getting him to raise fingers. They tried for toe movement too. His right toes would move, not his left. Nothing on the left side moved. When Laura inquired about surgery on his right leg, she was told that "neuro" still had not released David.

As David became more and more alert, efforts were made to stimulate him. Friends brought pictures. Between visits Laura would take them to the camera shop down the street to have them enlarged. They hung them in the room and held them up for David to see. They called out the names of the people pictured. At first, David seemed confused, but then he began to raise his finger, if Laura said the right name. They brought David's favorite foods for him to sniff. They brought tapes of his favorite music and let him listen with earphones. They laughed and sang. One particular evening when the cassette player was humming, Laura pushed the speaker button to see what was playing. At the same time the melodious notes of James Taylor's *Fire and Rain* rolled out, Laura locked eyes with Chris, one of David's closest friends, and as the tears rolled down these faces, they heard those marvelous words that were the perfect fit for this situation. (At the time of printing copyright permission to print these words had not been obtained. Please listen to the song for the full effect). So David began to come around. Praise the Lord.

Laura spent hours explaining to David that he would be all right. She explained that he was in the hospital with a hurt leg. He would be okay soon. Yes, there had been a slight bump up with his car, but she had received a letter from a body shop asking to fix it. (This was true and totally laughable.) He could not talk right now because he had a tube in his throat, but it would be out soon. There was nothing wrong with his voice, so he would be able to talk when it was removed. They tried to communicate with David by having David blink or raise a finger. David seemed to be the only one who could keep the signals straight. On Saturday David underwent another Bronchoscopy.

On Saturday evening David appeared to be trying to pop his knuckles, a habit Laura had always discouraged, and she recognized it immediately. "He's trying to pop his knuckles! If he can do that, he might be able to write." Glances were exchanged and Laura grabbed a pen and paper. She carefully positioned the paper under David's hand. What would she find out? Did she want to know what she was about to discover? Now we need something easy for David to write. David held the pen and made some scribbles. Laura showed him the results. I need to line up your hand and the paper better and we'll try again."

Jeff said, "Make a 'C'."

David made the most beautiful 'C' she had ever seen. The small crowd cheered.

Immediately, more was wanted. Laura said, "What's another easy letter?"

As everyone was trying to think, David took the pen and wrote, 'David McDowell.' Then he wrote, "I love Beverly." And drew a heart. And again, in trauma, there was uncontrollable joy! It was an answered prayer to be able to communicate with David.

In the chapel the next day Laura sat with an apple that was to be her lunch, school make-up work for Dylan, and a stack of bills. She began her long prayer with these words, "Dear Heavenly Father, I come to you to give thanks for David's progress and to insure you that the glory for this miracle will be all yours. I come with some other worries in my hands, and ask if we could have a good long talk."

Sunday was a day of mixed blessings. Dianne went home. She had been there for two weeks, a constant companion, the strongest support a person could ask for. Laura was going to be lost without her. But her husband and two sons were coming home from a three-week hunting trip in the backwoods. They had only found out about David on Saturday. Dianne got in touch with them to see to it that they flew into Charlotte, rather than Raleigh. They were terribly upset with the news and came straight to the hospital. They all, including Dianne, spent the night at Catherine's. Laura realized she would have to get use to doing more on her own. Fortunately, she still had Jayne and Alex to help her out. She still had no car. Whenever she left the hospital, it was just to go to the parking lot or to grab a quick meal with a friend. Once, Jayne had taken her to Alex's where they washed her clothes and Laura took a shower. Jennifer had sent Laura a change of clothes and she had acquired a sweater and pillow from Catherine.

Sunday evening Dylan came to her rescue. Laura was upset at Dianne's leaving and Dylan, as he so often could do, sensed his mother's despair. "Come on Mom, I know what you need to do. This will make you feel better. I've been doing this a lot. We are going to see the babies!"

"Do you know where they are?"

"Yes, I know where everything is, but you don't want to go to the morgue. Tomorrow we will go talk to the helicopter pilots."

Off they went and Dylan was correct. What a show! There must be ten babies, all shapes and sizes and colors. If that does not put a smile on your face, it would have to be made of stone. What a joy to be with Dylan. He loved his brother so much that you could watch his face and know how David was doing. He was around for every prayer and every visit and he had not left the hospital, either. Dylan had attempted some schoolwork, but Laura wasn't pushing that. He saw to his mother's needs as his own. It was lonesome on the floor that night without Dianne. Dylan crawled under a chair to keep the light out of his eyes and Laura did the same.

The next morning the waiting room group voted Laura to be the second loudest snorer. It was a position she accepted with pride because she had no choice and she was ever so grateful for the sleep.

Laura sat a little longer in the cafeteria and paid some bills. She made a plan for getting her car to the hospital, although she had no idea if she would be able to drive it. She received a call from First Citizens bank that an account was being set up in David's behalf. Cindy, from the bank, said people had expressed an interest in helping and figured this was the best way. 'Who? What people?' thought Laura. Miracles were happening. She was still walking around with bridge club money and other donations. Some had been spent on food, but not much. In fact, not that much eating had taken place.

That evening, one of David's friends brought them supper. Jeff, Dylan, and Laura ate it together in the cafeteria. Another friend tried to deliver Laura's car. Unfortunately, someone left with his keys so he had to drive her car back home.

On Tuesday, Laura received her car. There was also a visit from a lady at Charlotte Institute of Rehabilitation. She explained what C.I.R or "Rehab" would be like. "Excuse me," Laura inquired, "Are you telling me that someone is making plans for David to go to Rehab?"

"Yes, but only if that is what you desire for David."

"Mercy, I wouldn't have him go any other place. They taught a friend of mine how to walk after a terrible wreck when I was in high school. What I'm saying is that, if someone is considering Rehab, then someone must think David is going to live."

"Yes, someone thinks that or I wouldn't be here. I was here before, but from his vital signs then, I didn't think I would be back. I'm glad I am."

"Well, this is the very best news! I'll be looking forward to working with everyone in Rehab. Look at me smile. Do you know about his leg? He is supposed to have surgery on it some time."

"No, I don't have any information about his leg."

Laura and Dylan celebrated this day by visiting with the helicopter pilots. One lady said that the entire office said a prayer for David as he was coming to them. Laura knew that she was living every mother's nightmare.

During the evening visit on Wednesday, Laura was tending to one of David's friends that had passed out. It was not the first time that someone hit the floor from the sight of David's condition. The Friday night nurse came down the hall. He stepped in to make sure everything was under control and shared a story with Laura. "Last night I was in here with David. The guy from respiratory came up to check the machine, lines, pressure and all those things. I told him that David could write his name. He said, 'No way. There is no way that someone with a head injury as bad as David's could write his name.' Watch I said, and I'll show you. Well, he just couldn't believe it! Then I tried something else. I said, 'David, David, I want you to answer something for me. Show me the fingers, if you know. If you don't know, don't worry about it, because it's just a game. Do you know what two times two is?' David held up four fingers! We were so excited that we couldn't stand it and I wanted you to know." Laura couldn't stand it either. When David's friend was able to go and transportation was taken care of for a safe trip home, Laura shared the news of the nurse's discovery. She also spent some time asking some math questions of David. To her this showed a lot of processing, recall, and logic going on in her young man's head. What relief. What joy! Making 11 o'clock phone calls was fun this night.

Dylan had made other sleeping plans too. Jeff had taken to sleeping in his car. Dylan took his mom up to Pediatric Intensive Care. Actually, if David had not been 6'2", this is where they would have been the entire time. The doctors felt that David needed the adult bed. What a treat! There were recliners up here in pediatrics. There was even a shower! Laura went back downstairs to retrieve her blanket, but Jeff had given it away. Same old, same old story. Anyway, the shower was great and the recliner was great. What was not great was that the world-champion snorer of all time was two recliners away. Hopefully, the next night would be better.

On Thursday, Laura was told that David would soon be moving to progressive-neuro. This would still provide excellent care, but not as intense as ICU. He would be in a ward with his own nurse, but not necessarily a private-duty nurse. To Laura, this meant that David had passed his crisis and would live. Then she was told that "neuro" had released David to "ortho" and someone would be coming to talk to Laura about David's leg. Wow!

A fine gentleman showed up that afternoon from not "ortho", but "plastics". He explained that David's leg would require two things. One, muscle must be removed from somewhere on David and grafted to the exposed bone site. Then, skin needed to be removed from somewhere on David and grafted to the muscle. There was no doubt as to the seriousness of this procedure. Without the live muscle, the bone would not receive nutrients to heal and David would lose his leg. Several muscles and skin sights must be examined. The best muscle for the size and lack of detriment to David would be from the back of the leg. It would take the brain about two weeks to retrain that muscle to move in the opposite direction. The ideal skin site would also be on that leg. That way, all wounds would be together for treatment. It made sense to Laura. She asked if things were more a risk since his leg had been exposed for two weeks. "Well, normally we like to take care of things right away, because there is always a chance for infection. In this case there has been no infection. If David's muscle in the back was bruised in the wreck, it has now had two weeks to heal. There is actually a better chance now that we will be able to use it," This was good news, Laura thought. "We will run some tests, look at some x-rays, check the schedule in the operating room and get back to you."

This was turning into another eventful day. Laura went upstairs with Dylan to check out the waiting rooms for progressive-neuro. They were smaller with the same horrible chairs. It did not look like there was enough room to stretch out on the floor. It was beginning to dawn on Laura that sleeping on the floor was not as necessary as it had been. They did not provide blankets, etc. for the families of patients in progressive-neuro, although the visiting hours were pretty much the same. Laura decided that maybe it was time to take the car out for a few spins to make sure she could still drive. Jeff had located a place to stay for free across the street. He just had to be inside for the night by ten PM. Laura had some extra options because she had relatives in town. Some plans needed to be made. When Dr. Caplin got back to Laura, she was back in the ICU waiting room. He said that he would not be able to book the surgery unit until Sunday. They were able to use the muscle from David's leg and surgery was set for seven AM Sunday morning. They would come for David around six in progressive-neuro and bring him back. The surgery should take about two hours and he would come to the surgery waiting room afterwards to talk. There was a different waiting room for everything.

Laura was still sitting in the waiting room when a nurse came in for her. She was from maternity. She was in fact, the cousin of the next-door neighbor of Laura's sister-in-law. Her cousin had called her to look up Laura. She said she had a wonderful surprise. She had a bed for her upstairs. "Maternity is so quiet. We have about ten empty beds. You can have a bed and a shower and Dylan can sleep in the recliner in the same room. The only restraint is to vacate by the next shift which comes on at seven." Laura could not believe her ears. She left word where she could be found and she and Dylan took off. Now, how about a nice warm shower before beddy-bye? Gosh, what heaven. Dylan settled down with the remote. Laura cautioned him not to make too much noise and not to stay up too late. We need to really take advantage of this. We can get six hours sleep. Just when they thought it couldn't get better; the nurse brought in heated blankets.

The night flashed by. Laura was awakened quietly at 6:30. There stood this true lady of mercy with a tray of coffee, hot chocolate, and pastries. Laura cried from the very thought of the kindness.

Once they got back downstairs Laura learned that David was in progressive-neuro. She could see him at 9:30. This was a strange place.

It was one large room with about eight beds. Curtains could be drawn between them. There was very little privacy. There was one private room but David wasn't in it. A young man from the same county was in it. Although he had been wounded in the head during a drive by shooting, everything looked to be going well for him. He went to a high school not too far from David's. There was another teenager who had run her car into a house at 90 mph after having a few drinks. David was in a little cubbyhole at one end. He had a small window. Laura busied herself with the hanging of the pictures and balloons and other favorites. David was becoming more and more alert. He could write just about anything he wanted. He still had his trach tube and feeding tube. He was breathing from the trach tube without assistance, but it was well known that the oxygen was right at hand. The probes in his head were gone as were several of the monitors. He still wore the rubber foam and plastic boots to keep away, what was referred to as, "foot flop". His left arm was still in a splint, left leg still held a fixator from his hip to his knee and there was still the fixator in his right leg from the knee to the ankle. What a mess this precious child was. He was also a little high from the morphine. He seemed to be aware of the change and was very content to rest in his mom's presence.

Dylan now had an entire new area to investigate and he was hard at it. He was locating restrooms and possible sleeping spots.

Fridays were not usually high visit days. There was school and ball games. This was one of those quiet Fridays. Laura was glad. She was trying to organize and get her thoughts together. She knew that spending the night would be difficult at best. Dylan had been invited to go out of town with his best friend. Not for tonight, but for tomorrow night. Laura was supporting this for Dylan. David's surgery was Sunday and she would be at the hospital at the crack of dawn. Jeff seemed to be floating in and out. She decided to try spending the night at home, if she could remember how to get home, see to Dylan's needs, be at the hospital all day Saturday, and spend Saturday night in Charlotte with friends or relatives. That way she could get to the hospital early without a long drive.

What a strange experience to drive home that evening. It was late. There was a box of groceries by the front door from a good friend. News had traveled of the surgery and the first night at home. Bucky and the groceries needed some attention. Laura packed a bag for Saturday and Sunday. They hit the sack as soon as they could. It was more than a little weird to sleep in one's own bed after such a long time and after such an ordeal. It felt good, but it was such a mixed blessing having David and not having David. Dylan eventually crawled in bed with Laura and then they both rested better.

The next morning brought mega-activity. See to Bucky and the other animals. Make sure Dylan has everything he needs. Enjoy that shower. Wash some clothes. Throw out some trash. Put up some things from the hospital. Grab the mail. Make sure there are things to work on while waiting. Get it together. Take Dylan to his friend's. Yes, they will bring him to the hospital tomorrow evening. Go. Be at the hospital for the 9:30 visit.

She dropped Dylan off. She already missed him. She missed Dianne. She missed David. Lonesome would be the word for this if things were normal. Would she ever see that wonderful normal again? How could anyone deal with this were it not for the Lord?

Saturday went well. David seemed to be adjusting to his new place. Actually, he was mentally in and out. He wrote a little and occasionally indicated pain. Laura spent the night at Alex's. It was his turn to wake her up. Relatives had just about paid their dues.

Laura arrived on Sunday in time to see David and tell him not to worry. He was more than drowsy when he left the room. Laura realized that she was spending this day with Jeff. Dr. Caplin came to visit after the surgery. "Every thing went very well. We were able to do the muscle and skin grafts. It looks really good."

"What will happen if this does not work?" inquired Laura.

"I believe we have a 95% chance for success. Let's just go with that for now." He winked at Laura. She knew what was in the wink. She knew that David's leg was still in jeopardy.

It wasn't long before Laura and Jeff were able to go back to see David. He could nod his head in response to their questions. He could let them know if he was still in pain. It seemed like hours before David was released to return to his room. This had been a very long day. Dylan showed up in time to see David for a few minutes and then they headed home.

Laura and Dylan had discussed several times his returning to school. He had missed twelve days of school. He had done some make-up work, but not enough. Dylan was smart. He usually managed A's and Laura wasn't really worried. She knew that in good time, with the teachers at CMS, Dylan would be fine. There was no way this child could have functioned at school, but after a little break and a night in his own bed, maybe it was time. Laura talked with Dylan about giving school a shot for tomorrow. He seemed hesitant, but willing to try. Laura said that since they were getting home so late, they would sleep late and she would get Dylan to school about 9, then head to the hospital for 9:30 visit. She would leave the hospital after the 1:30 visit and pick Dylan up from school. They would return to the hospital for the 5:30 visit, eat supper, do homework, visit at 8:30 and then, return home. For some reason Laura felt that she could keep up this schedule. When everything calms down, maybe we can find you a ride home from school and on some days you won't have to come to the hospital.

The next morning was completely impossible for Dylan. He got so upset in front of the schoolhouse that there was no way he could go inside and make a success of the day. After thirty minutes of total tears, he went to the hospital with Laura. Laura was very much aware that both she and Dylan had broken hearts.

It was October 12th. David was still groggy from the surgery and still progressing out of his coma. He continued to move his right leg and arm. That day he had twelve visitors, ten of his very best friends and two teachers. Sandra came again and this time she did not faint. David communicated as best he could with notes. He still could not talk due to the trach. Around four "ortho" doctors showed up, represented by a very knowledgeable and fine man. "We've been told that 'plastics' is done and now 'ortho' is holding up the show. We don't want to be the ones keeping David from going to Rehab so tomorrow we are going to remove the fixator from David's left leg and insert a rod from his hip to his knee inside the femur. This will allow him to put weight on his left leg before his bone is healed and help with his walking. The fixator will stay in his right leg, because those bones are not hollow and no rod is possible there."

Laura replied, "That sounds good, but he just had surgery yesterday. Is this too soon? What happens if the left fixator stays in awhile?"

"No, not too soon, his doctors have cleared him. He is a strong young man. This fixator is going through right much tissue. The longer it stays in, the better the chance for infection."

"Okay." And she signed the consent forms.

David was progressing nicely out of his coma. The next day, he realized that he was going to surgery and he cried. Laura comforted him the best she could. She held his head and his hand while wiping away his tears. She told him that he would be all right. She would be just outside the door and she knew that God had seen him through so much that there was no way He would let them down now. David cheered up. He left for surgery and Laura followed as closely as possible. When she was told that she could not continue she kissed David and headed for the Chapel, her home away from home. David did fine in surgery.

On October 14th nurses explained that David would be able to talk by adjusting the trach opening. He would breathe through his nose while talking. He had been given a "taste test" and he would be okay with solid food, but not liquids. His ventilator tube had weakened his ability to completely close off his lungs. So liquids could slip into his lungs and cause pneumonia. What news! Laura and Jeff encouraged David to talk, but he was afraid.

Later in the day, when Laura and David were alone, she tried to get David to speak again. She adjusted the tube. She said, "David, I know you want to talk. Don't be afraid. Please try."

His response came, "Why?"

Now, there are times in your life that you never forget. This was one of them. Laura had not heard her son speak in twenty-one days, and for most of that time was not sure that she ever would. Tears of joy. Tears of joy! Praise the Lord.

Laura went on to explain that he could quit writing notes. He could quit writing that he was the king of the hospital and he could start telling everyone, instead. "Wouldn't that be nice?"

"Yes." Came the reply. David was grinning from ear to ear and Laura was crying.

David said, "Mama" and grabbed her hand.

When Jeff and Dylan returned David said, "Dylan," "Dad," and "Thank you."

The preacher came in and David said, "Hello, Ben." When he left he said, "Thank you."

When Chris came in, David said that he looked like a "dog's butt" and he told everyone to buy him a hydraulic bed to have at home.

The next day they moved David to a regular room on the orthopedic floor, and Dylan was able to spend an entire day at school. One of David's friends picked Dylan up and brought him to the hospital every afternoon. Then Laura and Dylan would leave the hospital around ten and Jeff began spending the night in David's room. In the mornings Laura would drop Dylan off at school and head for the hospital. She and Jeff would switch off for supper. Dylan would do his homework. If Dylan was late for school, he missed part of math. Laura was a math teacher, so no problem.

Months later, David would share with Laura that he had an "out of body" experience while in this room. He could see the people in his room and was floating over them. On one evening in particular, David looked at Laura and said, "Steven Lawrence broke my legs."

Laura could not believe her ears because everyone had been told that it would be better for David not to discuss the wreck. "What?" she replied.

"Steven Lawrence broke my legs."

"How do you know that? Did someone in here tell you that?"

"No, the police told me."

"The police?" Now, Laura was getting confused because no police had been around David. There were firemen and rescue workers at the wreck, but no police had been around David then and none had talked to him at the hospital.

"Yes, the police were talking about it at the wreck."

"Did you hear anything else?"

"No, the lights were too bright."

Laura's heart froze for a moment as she thought, again, about how close her son had been to death.

On Monday, David was moved to Rehab, bed and all, through an underground tunnel. He could move only his right hand and leg. There was still no movement on the left side. They removed his feeding tube and his trach tube. The second day they put him in a private room.

Jeff moved into the room also. It was difficult for Laura to spend so much time with Jeff because she was still afraid of him, but there was no way that she was giving up any time with David. It really bothered her that Jeff made such a mess in the room and she felt the need to clean it up as soon as she arrived in the morning. Rachel, the custodian, also noticed this and made a few comments.

The therapists began on David immediately! There was a speech therapist, an occupational therapist, a physical therapist, recreational therapist, and a cognitive thinking specialist. At first they met with him in the room. They saw to his hygiene, got him dressed (Laura bought long pants with snaps on the sides and seamed underwear with Velcro for easy off and on access), exercised him and tested him until the cows came home. There was no spinal cord damage.

Once when David returned from therapy he announced that they needed to call Mrs. Smith. Laura asked him why. He replied, "Well, they asked me to tell them the months of the year and if I hadn't been able to sing that song she taught us in kindergarten, I would never have known the answer!"

David's IQ had dropped ten points or so and his sequencing skills were pretty bad, but he was able to relearn. He was retraining his brain with every experience, which made him very comfortable watching Sesame Street. His schedule began at seven with bathing and dressing, then therapy until twelve and again from one until four. At first he had a wheelchair with neck support, and then they ordered one for him with a great cushion ($450) and no neck support. David was getting stronger, but he still could not have liquids. Laura and Jeff were told that they could be with David during therapy as long as they did not interfere. On November 2$^{nd}$, David lifted his left leg!

David's room was completely covered from ceiling to floor with posters and cards from his friends. There was love everywhere he looked! There were plants and balloons. Laura bought a VCR so David could watch some movies. It was as if his brain was going from age six to sixteen right in front of everyone's eyes. He was starting to eat, which was a blessing after losing seventy pounds. David played electronic games and surfed the Internet looking for his next car. His friends took him in his wheelchair to visit around the hospital and outside for fresh air in the evenings. They brought him take-out food. Dianne came back to visit. On Sundays they went to church in the physical therapy room.

Bucky came to visit David in Rehab, too. David really enjoyed those times. Laura would give Bucky a mild tranquilizer that she got from the vet for the trip. Laura was tempted to take some herself, but she held back.

Laura was out of sick days. She called personnel to find out what to do. The doctors had been told that she needed to be with David to learn how to take care of him when he got home. Got home! What wonderful words. Personnel told Laura that she had more than forty sick days already donated to her from teachers. She was never to worry about when she was coming back.

Just in case they might make it, Laura ordered eight tickets including a handicap ticket for the State vs. Carolina football game the week before Thanksgiving. It was to be played about a mile from the hospital. She was hoping hard.

On November 5th, David stood up!

On November 6th, assisted by his therapist and Mom, David walked ten feet!

On November 8th, David moved his left arm and Channel Eight news came to the hospital to interview him. He was on the news that evening. His wreck, condition, and his room full of love were shared with the audience. David said, "Well, a lot of people said that I was not going to make it, but I did. And now, I'm just going to keep on going. I want to go home. I miss my family and my room and my friends. I miss going to school and to church." Laura got a chance to talk about the miracle and all the prayers.

The church held a private spaghetti dinner and a public hotdog sale for David. They raised $5000 for his medical bills.

David's pin sites from the fixator were fine and Laura cleaned them twice a day. He was graduating from having to use a slide board to get into the wheel chair to standing, taking a step, and sitting down. Mom was being trained on how to get him standing, the necessary rotation and finally the sitting. With the attachment of the wheelchair legs and placement of pillows, arm rests and straps, the process took twenty to thirty minutes. Getting the bathing and toiletries done in the bathroom was an unbelievable process.

David's right leg was not healing like it should. The doctors attached, what David called, "a vacuum cleaner", to his surgery site to promote circulation. After suffering severely through this for three weeks, David needed a second skin graft. Maybe this would be a blessing. Whenever his leg needed to be cleaned, David would shake with pain. He would bite his pillow and cry, but he would not scream.

By this time the social worker at the hospital had spoken to Laura and Jeff. Jeff was told, as was Laura, that neither parent could spend the night in David's room and neither could be there before nine in the morning. At one point Jeff told David that he did not have to go to therapy if he did not want to. When David tried this, there was a big stink and everyone got upset. Then Laura was told that she could not be there until eleven AM and Jeff could not be there until visiting hours. Both parents must be out of the room by 9PM.

Jeff did not handle this very well. In spite of the fact that he was keeping the room a mess, was interfering with therapy, trying to help the doctors when they came in, and at one point, whatever he was taking, caused him to pass out and fall on David's right leg, Jeff did not want to take orders from anyone. He just fussed and cussed and complained about the most excellent staff that Laura had ever seen.

David was uneasy the first night alone. Laura placed the phone within his reach and everything she could imagine that he could need on his tray.

On the day of the second plastic surgery Laura was sitting alone in the waiting room. Dr. Henry, the neurosurgeon, came by and stopped in front of her. He said, "David, right?"

"Yes," Laura replied.

"How is he doing?" Dr. Henry seemed almost stunned to see her. In fact, Laura was told later, that Dr. Henry had told the other surgeons during the surgery on September 23rd that they could have some time with David, but they should keep it short because David was not going to make it. He had a non-survivable brain injury.

"He is having his second plastic surgery to save his right leg. He is writing complete sentences with subject and verb agreement and correct punctuation. Two days ago he walked ten feet."

"Really? That's wonderful." Dr. Henry said slowly. Then just as slowly, he turned to his assistant and said, "Where were we going?"

"Plastics" told Laura that the surgery went well and he was soon back in his room. He would not be allowed out of bed for a week and was on complete bed rest for four days. That would hold up some of his therapies and cause a longer hospital stay, but saving his right leg was more than worth it. David was uncomfortable about having to regress and use a bedpan again, but it was doctor's orders.

Then Jeff made a bad mistake. David called him early the next morning to tell him that he had to go to the bathroom. Jeff sneaked into David's room, got him out of bed, and was on his way back to the bed with David when the nurse came in. She reported what she had seen to the doctor. Jeff refused to talk to the doctor. The doctor issued orders that Jeff was not allowed on the floor and security was posted to keep him out. Jeff had a pure fit, as did David. Laura was caught in the middle because David was so upset. She tried to explain hospital policy to David, but he could not understand. Finally, after two days of turmoil she said to David, "David, if you had a choice, would you choose to take a crap in front of everyone here or lose your right leg?"

David replied, "Take the crap."

"Okay," Laura explained, "That is the situation you are in. That was the last surgery possible to save your leg. It has to work. Your Dad knew this and still he chose to get you out of bed and risk your leg. The social worker has explained that they are trying to set things up like they will be at home. Your Dad does not live with us and there are very good reasons why he doesn't. Please try to understand what has happened here. Your Dad has gotten caught doing something wrong and he cannot deal with it. If he had allowed himself to talk to the doctor, he might not be in this mess and you would not be in this mess either."

David tried a little harder to deal with the situation and he began making great progress. His leg began to heal and his walking got better and better. Laura wheeled him down to the creek at lunch to feed the ducks. His friends kept coming. Beverly and Chris came almost every day. Laura realized that it was the middle of November and she had not bought the first Christmas present. While the kids were watching movies, she used the lights under David's bed to look through magazines and the phone to place orders. She would have used the Internet, but she could not get the computer away from David during the day. One Sunday, Laura left early to go to a night football game with Alex. It was the only time she left early or missed any time with David. Dylan and Chris were in charge and they would do fine. Once, when she had car trouble, she rented a car to make her visits. Once she had a kidney stone and counted her blessings when she finally passed in the middle of the night at home. She lost twenty-five pounds.

They came to Laura about a week before the State game. It was not yet decided if David would be going to the game or if he would be coming home for a visit the following weekend. Someone from Rehab would visit her house on Wednesday morning to suggest modifications for David's access.

So on Wednesday morning, Laura was up bright and early and had accomplished a major cleaning job. The man from Rehab walked through the house making suggestions about removing doors, which bathroom would be the best, what all was needed in the bathroom, how much the bed should be raised, where to put clothes in his room, the necessity of a fire escape from David's bedroom window, and several more adjustments. Then he lowered the boom. "David will do fine once he is inside the house. The problem is that he cannot get inside the house. The front is impossible because the steps are too high. The back is possible, but there is no way to get to it from the front drive." He made some suggestions and left. Laura stood helplessly in the driveway.

Jessica appeared from next door. "What's going on this morning?"

"That was the man from Rehab. There is a chance David could be here on Saturday, but he can't get into the house. I don't have a ramp and I don't have a driveway."

Jessica said, "Well, I was coming to tell you not to worry about a ramp. Gary is going to build you one."

"What? I can't let you do that."

"Yes, you can. Gary has to build them all the time with his construction projects. And besides, we have all that wood left over from our house that's in our basement. I've been after him to get rid of it. So it won't cost anybody anything. Don't say anymore about it. It's done. What else is wrong?"

Laura, who could not believe her ears, replied, "Well, there's the driveway and the inside things to change. The driveway needs to be extended to reach the back door."

Jessica said, "Okay, let's see. I have a friend that just got a driveway poured and she was very pleased with the work and the price. I'll go call her and see what she says. You be thinking about the inside and make a list of what you can do and what someone else needs to do."

Jessica was back in a flash. "There's a man coming over in about thirty minutes to look at this drive. He will give you an estimate and you can take it from there. Now, what about the other stuff? This time Jessica had her phone with her. Laura called her church. When Ben answered the phone, she explained some of her problems about the changes she needed, the slide for David's window, the open shelves for the bedroom and the doors that needed to be moved for David to make turns in his wheelchair. He came over and got the list. He said that the Methodist Men were looking for some way to help and they would be back in the morning to do the work.

Now, the truck pulled in the driveway. A gentleman got out and on his tee shirt was written, "Jesus Christ Saves." He measured the drive and gave Laura a quote that is at least $3000 less than she was expecting. He said, "I can come back this evening. I'm on another job right now but I can come back and mark it off. Then I can pour it tomorrow night. It will be close, but it should be plenty dry by Saturday morning."

Laura said, "Okay!" and showed him where the ramp would be. He said that would work and he would extend the drive up to meet it, but there was a problem. The dog lot was in the way and the corner of the fence would have to be moved. Laura said that she would see to that and the man was on his way. He didn't even want any "up front" money.

Laura looked at Jessica and said, "And some people think that there is no God. My driveway has been filled with angels all morning. I don't know about that fence. I'm supposed to be at Rehab in thirty minutes. I'll make some calls from there."

Jessica said, "No, put Bucky in the garage and I'll start making calls about the fence. Do you know anyone?"

"Not a soul. The fence was put in by Sears twenty years ago."

"Don't worry. Go tend to David. Call me in a little while."

Laura left for the hospital on a cloud. How can so many wonderful things happen out of such a disaster? David fussed at her for being a few minutes late. He was hungry. When she called Jessica after lunch, Jessica said, "You are not going to believe this. The first company I called was in Kannapolis. I was going straight down the line in the phone book. When the lady asked whom the fence was for, I started explaining about David's wreck. As soon as I mentioned his name, she stopped me. She said that her daughter was one of David's nurses in trauma and had kept them posted on David. They will be over this afternoon to fix the fence. How about that?!" How about that, indeed! God is in His Heaven and angels are here on earth.

As it turned out, David made it to the State vs. Carolina football game rather than taking the trip home. It was his first outing from the hospital.

Someone had to approve his going, but they did and none too soon. One of David's friends went with Laura to the hospital to help. They got David dressed and ready. They got him in the wheelchair, checked out and into the van. They got him out of the van and into the wheelchair and into the stadium. It was a glorious day! The rest of the friends, including two of Dylan's friends met them at the game. The sun shone and the crowds roared and the bands played. The girls in front had on short skirts. The guests got David all the food he could eat. He was exhausted by the middle of fourth quarter, and that was okay, because Carolina was winning, so they started back to the hospital. Instead of the trip home, everyone met in David's room. What a day! Praise the Lord!

Less than a week later, David left the hospital a second time to be at home for Thanksgiving. Laura was told that Jeff could not participate in this trip. He would only be able to see David during his regular visitation times as set up by the custody mediation once David was released from the hospital. Channel Eight filmed this event, too. They were at the hospital in time to watch Laura and Dylan help David into the car. They filmed David at home and Laura working on the dinner (with Dylan's help). The oven was full of food that had been delivered the day before from Caldwell Middle School. The meal was delicious. David went to his room around six. He wanted to see how his altered room would feel and then took in the changed bathroom access. By seven in the evening David was more than ready to return to the hospital for some rest.

On December 2$^{nd}$, David was released from the hospital. He was to return for outpatient therapy starting soon. Laura had been trained in transfers for the van and bathroom. They went home with chairs for the tub and commode. Now, it was up to her and David to continue therapy and not get discouraged. Laura was excused from work until at least January 6$^{th}$. The only limb that David could move with ease was his right arm. His right hand had a small fracture but David would not allow even a splint on it. He had to have something he could move. It was amazing that he could stand on two broken legs. His walking was limited to the parallel bars at Rehab. David's schoolwork would begin again with second semester. Hopefully, he would be able to salvage two credits from the fall. Two would be lost for sure. They had been loading up his room for several days so she would not have more than a car full on the big day. Laura went by herself. She worked very hard to get it and keep it all together. They took pictures of everyone, even some patients. Laura had to keep David busy until three to give his friends time to gather outside his home.

The next day there was an article in the tribune by Lance Morris. Lance was one of the people who told Laura that he had never prayed until he prayed for David. The article read:

> "When Laura McDowell announced friends could greet her son for as long as his strength would allow, one by one, hundreds of friends and classmates came forward, tears in their eyes, to hug and kiss David.
>
> After more than three months of hospitalization, recovering from a nearly fatal head-on collision in August (September), David McDowell finally came home for good Wednesday.
>
> Laura and David McDowell arrived at their home on Westside Drive under police escort. A crowd of more than 220 friends and classmates lined the street applauding, waving and holding up banners welcoming David home.
>
> As Laura McDowell pulled the van into the driveway, Bucky, the McDowell's dog, jumped and barked from behind the fence in anticipation.
>
> David Evens and Jimmy Norris, two of David's closest friends, led the crowd up the driveway to greet him.

Opening the passenger door, the frail 17 (16)-year-old appeared wearing sunglasses and a visor to shield his eyes form the sun.

During his time in the hospital he had numerous medical procedures to correct the damage to his legs and left arm. The process of rehabilitation is not over, according to Laura McDowell, and he may have to go to Rehab three times a week, she said. Norris and Evens lifted David's gaunt frame from the car and placed him into a wheel chair. Although the surgery and rehabilitation have been successful, David can walk a mere 15 feet on his own, according to Laura McDowell.

On the back of his head were two slight bald spots, from where his head had been shaved and there were slight traces of scars from a tracheotomy on his neck.

Weak, but happy to be home, David sat in his wheelchair as Laura McDowell turned him to face the crowd that had gathered at the top of the driveway.

'Well, he's home,' said Alice Evens, a long time family friend, and hundreds of teenagers cheered and clapped.

As the crowd quieted, the Rev. Ben Royal of Christ United Methodist Church, where the McDowell's are members, came forward. Royal, after greeting David with a hug, asked the people to bow their heads and pray.

'For several months, we didn't know if David would come home,' he said, as sobs broke the silence, 'but the Lord has blessed David, and has blessed us.'

The most tender greeting came from his younger brother, Dylan, who held David and kissed his cheek.

'He told us today that this was the best Christmas present ever,' said Alice Evens, referring to an earlier conversation with Dylan.

David, after having received hundreds of hugs and kisses, was wheeled up to a wooden ramp into his home.

'His favorite place is on the sofa in the living room, so that's where we're headed,' Laura McDowell said.

David, a man of few words, according to his mother, simply said 'Thank you'."

# At Home

A crowd of friends followed David into the house. They handed Laura the "Welcome Home" banner they were holding outside and all gathered in the living room. Channel Eight news came by in a few minutes and interviewed David and his friends. David showed them how he could stand by himself. Most people remained to see the TV cast before heading home. Once the gathering was reduced to one of David's friends and Jayne, one of Laura's, David reminded Laura that he was ready to go to Kabuto's for his homecoming dinner.

Reality was hitting Laura in the running lights. She was excited but pretty tired from the long day. She was worried that she might not be able to provide for all of David's needs. Every transfer took twenty minutes and had to be done exactly right. Any miscalculation on her part could land them on the floor and David back in the hospital. The only limb David could move was his right arm. Laura had to stop in moments like this and pray to the Lord for wisdom, courage, strength, and the peace that passes all understanding.

Transfers were one of the things that you never saw in the movies. In the movies everyone was all situated and comfortable. In real life that was not the case. First David had to be positioned correctly. Too far back or too far forward could cause a fall. The footrests of the wheelchair had to be removed so they would not be in the way. A transfer belt was fastened around David. Then Laura positioned one of her feet between David's and bent at the knees. She would hold onto the belt in back of David. David would put his right hand on her shoulder for support. On the count of three they would rise and for a second Laura supported all of David's weight. If everything seemed in balance then they would slowly rotate ninety degrees to the target. Laura would move her feet ever so slightly, nudging David's in a turn as she did. Then Laura would slowly lower David to the target seat. At first David could not stand and they used a "slide board" as a bridge between the two seats. If David was headed for the commode, it was also necessary to get his pants removed before he sat down. David could not help with this because he was holding on with his good arm and hand. If David was transferring to the bed or sofa, placement was very important. Once he was seated, then Laura would lift his legs into a comfortable position. Often it was still necessary for Laura to climb on the bed or sofa and adjust David by pulling on the bed pads that were always in place. The transfers in the bathroom were especially difficult because they either had to do two of them, using the bath seat as a stopping point, or they had to do a one-eighty. Once David got a little stronger he could use his right hand to steady himself at the sink.

Laura transferred David to the bathroom. This was very intense because it was so complex. Then Laura dealt with underwear and positioning for David to be comfortable. Poor David. It was very humiliating for him and he was so brave.

They transferred back to the wheelchair, to the car, and out of the car to Kabuto's. The wheelchair fit at the table so they could relax. The waiter said, "Hey Man, I just saw you on TV!" and he brought David a free appetizer. It was a marvelous dinner. By the time Laura got David into bed they had made 19 successful transfers. All meds were administered and David's pin sites were cleaned. David slept in his own bed for the first time in three months. The night passed without incident.

One of the best ways to hold anxiety at bay is to have a good routine. Laura set about this the next morning. She got up and got Dylan ready. She checked with David to make sure he was okay and took Dylan to school. When she returned she got David to the bathroom for bathing, dressing, and pin cleaning. It was very important to clean all the pin sites of the fixator at least twice a day. This kept the skin from growing up around them and causing infection and pain. Laura moved David to the living room sofa, turned on the TV and fixed breakfast. Things had changed in David's eating habits and filling him up was a challenge. He needed to regain seventy pounds. He would have a snack about ten and lunch around one. Laura would pick up Dylan and they would all have a snack. The house would be filled with friends for the rest of the day. Laura cooked as many meals as she could, but more than once she needed to pick up food.

Bedtime for David began at nine. If he went to sleep on the sofa, Laura was afraid to wake him up for bed. Unless he was wide-awake, it was much too dangerous to try to move him. The few times that he went to sleep Laura slept on the love seat until he woke up. She was not going to leave him in case he rolled off the sofa and onto the floor.

Not many days after David came home Annie passed away. She was still keeping some children at the time. It was very sad for Laura, David, and Dylan. They had grown very close over the years. The funeral was held at the church. It was the next place David went.

The hospital called to say that David was set up for rehab in January. After a few days at home Laura called them back. She fully realized that even though they were doing exercises, she was no therapist. She requested an earlier date. After all, David was not going back to school and she was not returning to work until January 6th. Sitting around like this was great, but no progress was being made and probably should be while they had some free time. The next week they began rehabilitation for an hour a day. Getting to rehab took an hour and a half counting transfers and the same to come home. They ate an early lunch on the way and got a snack on the way back. This really filled up their time and it was good for everyone concerned.

Laura tried to focus on Christmas because it was just around the corner. It was scary leaving David because he could not get to the bathroom by himself. Laura would always take Dylan's pager, make sure Dylan and someone else was with David, and make very short trips. Mostly, she bought electronics at Sears for Christmas. Alex asked if there was anything he could do. She asked him to please buy two trees and bring them over. For some reason he never got this done, so one day after Rehab she and David stopped for trees. Laura was learning to do even more on her own. Of course, once the trees were home, there was lots of help getting them in the house. Laura decorated as she could. Alex came over a few times and took her to dinner. It was very tense trying to eat and listen for the pager.

Steven got into some more trouble and was suspended from school. Most people thought that he did not want to be at school when David returned.

One day there was an ice storm predicted for the late afternoon and evening. Laura and David decided to try therapy anyway. They should have plenty of time to get home before the storm. Not true. On the way home the car started making a strange noise. Laura pulled over on the side of I-85 and got out to look under the hood. David had instructed her to look for a torn belt and, lo and behold, there was one with a big tear in it. The noise was caused by the lose part flapping all around and hitting things. David said that it would continue to split. Well, there they sat. Laura was just beginning to realize her predicament; ice coming down, child who could not walk, and no way to communicate.

Seconds before Laura went into a total panic, a tow truck pulled off the road in front of them. A gentleman got out and introduced himself. He asked if she needed help. This surely had to be an angel. He went to a church in Caldwell and was a friend of some people who knew David and Laura. This wonderful man helped Laura to get David to his truck. He had to lift him into the cab. Then he hooked up the car and took them to Drye's garage where he would accept no money. The belt was replaced and soon Laura was on her way home again. The Lord was still in charge. Praise the Lord.

Christmas came. Jeff came by to see the boys and did not stay long. Friends came over for dinner. Alex helped to grill sixteen steaks for the crowd. It was a grand and glorious birthday celebration for Jesus!

January 6th came really soon. Laura got up at five and got herself ready. She tended to David's needs from 6 until 7. Laura would take David to school and then come home, pick up Dylan and take him to school before going to work. After a few days, Jimmy began coming by to take David to school. Laura would pick David up at noon and they would head to therapy. Jimmy would pick Dylan up and bring him home. In the evenings Miss Collins came by to home-school David in Algebra III and U S History. David was taking three subjects in school and getting credit for weight training because he was in therapy every day. In the end this would mean that David would only lose two credits due to the wreck. David was relearning everything. Life was getting better.

David was gaining weight and getting stronger. His physical therapy was really helping and the transfers were getting easier. It was almost to the point that he could bathe himself. He started asking at Rehab about driving. His doctor said that he would have to wait a year. David slipped quickly into some depression and made this comment, "Why am I the one who can't drive? I did not cause this wreck. I'm only doing all this therapy so I can walk out to my car and get in it and drive."

Laura was pretty upset. The head injury was the problem. She understood that the doctors were waiting to make sure that David would not have seizures and was physically able to drive. It did not help the situation with David and she could not allow him to give up. She already knew of one person who had been in the hospital at the same time as David and was now dead because he had given up.

Steven had a court date. Laura did not go to court. Her cousin, who was representing her, told her to go to work and let Jeff go to court. The judge would more than understand that she needed to be at work. Steven received a $50 fine for driving without a license and a 30-day suspended sentence. He received a $200 fine for driving with reckless endangerment and another 30-day suspended sentence.

David's birthday was coming up on February 5th. Laura, Jimmy, and Dylan plotted to buy David a car. David had seen this car once before and David had shown it to his Mom once coming back from Rehab. It was an electric blue 1973 Chevrolet Impala with chrome wheels and hydraulics. Chris stayed with David while Laura, Jimmy, and Dylan went after the car. It was not the best deal in the world because it had major problems, but it got the job done. Jimmy took the car home and stayed up all night making a big bow for the hood.

David had not smiled for two weeks. The car turned him around. When Laura brought him out of the house the next morning and he saw Jimmy pulling up the driveway in his birthday present, he grinned from ear to ear. It was worth all the problems to see that smile on David's face. From then on, Jimmy would drive his truck to Laura's and then drive David to school in the new car. David got a license tag that read "HopaSmrf ".

This car was the exact "carrot" that Laura was looking for. It got David up off the sofa and into auto-parts stores, onto the Internet, and in a car club. He began doing what work he could on the car and doing a lot of research planning for things he could not do, not yet anyway. One of Laura's most fond memories was looking out the kitchen window one morning. The month was May and David was just starting to come out of his wheelchair. She looked out and saw the hood up on the car. David was standing up leaning against the front of the car and Dylan was sitting on the engine following David's instructions very carefully. What a scene.

Financially, there was mostly good news. Laura had good major medical insurance. She was very thankful that she had gone with that rather than an HMO. She had also taken out a disability policy that had an accident policy attached to it. The accident policy gave her enough money to take care of enough bills not to put her house in danger. People were very kind to Laura. Many people just sent her a check to help. The two insurance companies involved both paid David 100%. It was to David's benefit not to collect the entire amount at once, but to spread it out over his lifetime. So, when the check came in, David paid Daniel (who would only take part of the one-third that was normal), paid the rest of the medical bills, and saved the rest for a more reliable car. The people at Jeff's Mother's church had a fundraiser for David, but the money never made it to David or Laura. Once Jeff said that he had some extra money that month and he wanted to give Laura some money for the medical bills. When Laura got the check it was for $50. The medical bills for the first twenty-four hours surpassed $175,000. Laura quit counting and did the best she could. She turned her financial problems over to the Lord.

She took out an ad in the paper thanking everyone for their help and support. She listed as many names and business as she could possibly bring to mind.

In January and February Laura was not able to talk to Dianne as much as she would have liked. Dianne and Charles went on about three weeks of vacation. They were hunting in Canada. When Laura talked to her in February she commented to David later, "I don't think Dianne really understands what is going on here. She made some suggestions that just can't be done. I sure wish she could come up here so she could see how things are going." Laura really missed her sister. She missed seeing Uncle

Don and her Charlotte kinfolks. She just put on her blinders and kept going.

David had his first nerve block. He really should have had it before he left the hospital but the doctor and therapist had some discussion about it and they decided to wait and see if the weight that David was applying to his leg would make it unnecessary.

It did not.

David had a botox nerve block in his arm and a phenol nerve block in his leg. It was extremely painful. Laura watched as they put six-inch needles in David and then moved them around until they got the most noise on the machine. At that point they injected the medicine. David was better, but his foot and leg were sending pain signals for weeks. It was like he had burning skin. It was a real trick getting a sock on his foot without hurting him too badly.

# Celebrating Life

The "windy" month of March was just that. David's therapy was changed to two days a week, two hours a day, just in time. Laura was out of sick days. She earned 2.15 annual leave days a month. That would cover the two afternoons a week that she would be taking David to therapy. David still had no use of his left arm and hand, but his legs were getting stronger. He could walk a few steps completely on his own.

On the days that David did not go to therapy Laura would pick him up at lunch and see him safely home. Then she would return to work. Jimmy would pick up Dylan.

Once Laura made a trip to the store and when she returned David was on the floor in the hall. He had tried to get to the bathroom by himself and fallen on the floor. He was not hurt, but they were in a pickle as to how to get him up. They took it in small steps; first to a stack of books, then to the ottoman, and finally to the wheelchair. As scary as it was a good plan had been formed in case it ever happened again.

It was on a Wednesday night that Kevin called and life took another sudden turn. Laura knew from the sound of his voice that something was terribly wrong. He said, "Aunt Laura, Mom is in the hospital. She is really sick. She has a brain tumor. They are working real hard to try to shrink it and get her stabilized. She will come home for the weekend to be with her family and have surgery on Monday. Can you come down?"

"Yes, of course I can. I'll get organized tonight, pack tomorrow, and leave Friday afternoon. Is there anything else I can do? Can I make some phone calls?"

"Dad has called Walt, but please call some other family members."

"Sure. Now tell me what has happened."

"Dad and I were in Arizona at a business show. When we called home last night Brad said that Mom was not feeling well and had some memory loss. Dad told him to call an ambulance and get her to the hospital. When Dad talked to the doctor the doctor said, "Come home immediately. Do not drive. Leave your truck and fly home. You might not make it. She has a very large tumor."

"Oh my God, Kevin, I am so sorry. I will see you on Friday."

David was on the sofa looking at his Mom in stunned silence. Laura explained the situation to him and asked, "Do you think that you are up for this trip?" David had not managed a ride for more than the 30 minutes it took to get to Rehab. It was four hours to Wilmington.

"Sure."

"I have to make some phone calls and get my act together. We have a lot to do to get ready. Dylan should be able to help. We need to get someone to help with Bucky."

Laura and David said a prayer for Dianne.

In a few minutes Dylan came in. Laura had to tell him that his favorite relative, his most supportive relative, his most fun relative was so very sick. She was really counting on Dylan to help her with some packing and getting things to the car. All of David's medical equipment would have to go. But Dylan was very upset because his little world kept crashing all around him. He went to his room and crammed his fist into the wall. They spent the rest of the night at the hospital getting his broken hand mended and set.

Alex said that he wanted to go with them and do the driving. Somehow they made it through therapy, school, work and left on Friday afternoon to pick up Alex and head out. The van was packed full. David sat in the front with Alex. Laura sat in the back with Dylan. It was a long, long, trip. They stopped for dinner and that involved a couple of transfers for David. Alex was getting the real picture. They headed straight for the hospital.

Dianne was confused but said that she was feeling better. She was glad about going home for the weekend. She was very glad to see Laura. She was not in pain. She told Laura that a couple of people in her office had the flu so when she started feeling bad she just thought she had it too. She had some trouble getting the checks done but did not think anything about it. Brad had been gone for the weekend and she did not want to be a damper on his good feelings on Monday so she did not say anything to him about feeling bad. She took him to his college class and when she got home she could not remember how to get back into her house. Laura had a migraine once and lost her memory for thirty minutes or so. It was real scary. She said that she tried one key and it did not work. She got back in the car and sat with the sun on her face for a few minutes and then she took a little nap. When she woke up she was fine and could remember how to get into the house. Later she picked Brad up but did not tell him until the next day about her strange experience.

Other people came to the hospital. Laura's group went to Dianne's and she got the boys settled. Dylan said that he would be in charge of David and would see him through the night. David promised to stay on the sofa and, yes, he had plenty of urinals. Alex took Laura back to the hospital where she stayed with Dianne overnight. Then he headed for his condo, which was about thirty minutes away.

It was a long night. Dianne did not sleep well. The patient next door kept banging things. It sounded like he was rebuilding the room. Nurses kept a constant check on Dianne. Laura was a big bundle of worries. She worried about her precious sister and her precious sons. She prayed for her sister and her sister's family; for David and Dylan; for strength and wisdom and peace.

At last it was morning and time to prepare Dianne for going home. Charles came with clothes. Everyone was feeling good about the weekend. The doctors were very satisfied with Dianne's progress.

There were a lot of people at Dianne's that day, lots of cousins and good friends dropping by. They decided on barbequed chicken, an old family favorite, for dinner. Dianne made out the grocery list and sent Laura shopping. David and Dylan were starving most of the time. Once Laura headed out to pick up some snacks for them and Charles said that they were spoiled. Alex came and helped with the cooking. Charles's attorney was there with many papers for Dianne to sign.

Sunday was a calmer day. They ate food that friends and neighbors brought in and just spent time visiting. Dianne and David had some nice time together. She was encouraging him about trying new things (like their shower) and he was making her feel better about the surgery. Dianne said to David, "I don't know why I have to have this thing in my head. I don't know why everyone is so upset. I have had more good years and blessings then most people have if they live to 105. I am fine. I am a Christian and that's what being a Christian is all about."

The surgery lasted a long, long time but went well. When the doctor came to the waiting room, Charles called about ten people into the room so everyone could hear the results at once. The doctor said that they could only remove about two-thirds of the tumor. It had tentacles that were reaching to the back of her brain. They removed most of her frontal lobe on one side so it would have room to grow. Normally a person with a tumor this size had about six months to live. They would start radiation treatments immediately but it was time to consider quality of life for Dianne.

It was a few more hours before anyone could see Dianne. When Laura and David and Dylan got their chance she was sitting up in the bed talking! She asked if the scar was too bad and Laura said, "No." It went from about an inch behind her ear over the top of her head and down the other side. There were big staples in it. Her head was shaved, but just to the middle of her head. Actually, it was a horrible sight, one that Laura would never forget, but Dianne would never know. Dianne said that she still had no pain but she did have double vision. The doctor told her that her vision would be bad for about four weeks. They kissed her and hugged her and talked about coming back. She would be in the hospital for a week or more so they planned to see her in two weeks.

There was a big snowstorm headed over the mountains and should be on top of them by morning so they drove home that night. Alex was beside himself by the time they got to his house. It was late. Everyone was tired. Some people handle that better than others.

The storm never made it so Laura, David, and Dylan made it to work and school the next day.

David continued to get stronger and to improve. Transfers were becoming easier because he could help. Laura still got up at five to make sure everything was on schedule and Jimmy continued to take David to school. Laura would pick David up on Tuesdays and Thursdays and take him to therapy. Therapy was from 2 to 4 so they had time to pick up some lunch on the way. Then they could get home in time for supper and settle down for tutoring and homework. Laura talked with Dianne and saw Alex when she could. She encouraged David to work on his car and Chris would take David to shop for auto parts. They were very busy.

Laura bought tickets to the Jimmy Buffett concert. It was very difficult to get eight tickets and two of them being handicap seats but Laura did not give up until the job was done. The concert was in June in Raleigh. Since they would be departing from different locations, Laura took Dianne's tickets to Wilmington when they went for Easter.

David underwent a bone graft to help his leg heal. Laura was concerned about disturbing the precious skin grafts but was reassured that everything would be all right. It was. Even though they were told that bones do not have nerves and can't feel pain, David was uncomfortable for quite a while.

Easter was the wonderful event that it was expected to be. Laura's family spent four days with Dianne. Alex came too. Laura made Easter baskets for all the boys and one for Dianne. "This is the first Easter basket I've had in thirty-five years and I'm going to eat every bit of it! This looks like one of the baskets some of my flowers came in."

"It is." Laura replied, "I saved it and several others from the things Charles wanted to throw out."

"Good. If I find something in this basket that I really like, I'm going to look in Kevin's and Brad's baskets to see if they have any. I might eat theirs too."

Charles returned from church just in time to join in the private church service going on at the kitchen table. Laura had read the entire story of the Crucifixion and was just beginning the prayer. The tape player was set for the Hallelujah Chorus. It was a good thing the player was set because at the end of the prayer there was not a dry eye. The music was a welcome relief and a true celebration. Alex rang the doorbell and Laura went flying. It was time to get dressed and begin the preparation for the feast. All morning long Laura had alternated rolls between Mary (getting ready for the Lord's word) and Martha (getting ready for dinner). When all was said and done, Mary had won, but the dinner also appeared on time. Trust in the Lord.

Charles told Laura later, "You know, for all these years, I could not figure out how you could deal with everything that was put before you, but now I know. I have never heard a more beautiful prayer. I am just beginning to know how much you trust in the Lord."

"It's the only way I am still alive," was her reply.

Dianne still encouraged David to try new things. She talked about her radiation treatment and the mask that they made for her to wear.

Laura had been to Wilmington to see Dianne eight times since March. Memorial Day weekend was especially nice. Charles drove the 4-wheel drive out onto the sand. David stretched out for a good sunbathe. Dianne sat under the umbrellas. Dylan ran up and down the beach and in and out of the water. It was a heaven-made day for sure. When the jellyfish appeared everyone packed up and headed for the movie. There were no stings because this group had learned a long time before not to mess with jellyfish. That night the celebration continued with steaks on the grill. What a perfect day!

The next week Dianne went out on her jet ski without incident. She experienced some nausea a few days later and her anti-inflammatory medicine was resumed. All in all, her health was holding and expectations for the concert were building.

On Thursday Charles had a dentist appointment in Charlotte so he brought Dianne and Brad with him. While he was at the dentist Dianne waited at her Aunt Cathy's house. It gave some relatives a chance to see Dianne without driving four hours to Wilmington. Laura, David, and Dylan joined them about five and the whole crew gathered for dinner at seven. Altogether there were nineteen people. It was a festive occasion, indeed! Alex joined them, Uncle Don, Aunt Helen, several sets of cousins and spouses and dates. Laura asked Charles about the most recent MRI and his face fell, just for an instant, and he did not recover quickly enough with the "It was fine" for Laura not to sense that something was amiss.

Sure enough, Laura had not been home more than ten minutes when Alex pulled up in the driveway. She was still checking messages when Alex came in the door. "I know that I've got some bad news. Let me get the rest of these messages and we'll go into the kitchen and talk." It had to be really bad because Alex had never showed up at her house without previous plans being made.

Laura walked into the kitchen and sat down. She knew that when someone suggested that you sit down, you probably needed to. Now no one even had to tell her. "Okay, I'm ready."

"Charles did not want to tell you this and then have you drive home. He was afraid you might be too upset. Now, I will just say it. The scan showed that the radiation has had no effect on the tumor. Dianne will have more surgery and very quickly and there might not be a Buffett concert. Charles does not know when the surgery will be, but it could be as early as Saturday. He should get a call tomorrow around lunch."

"Okay. I'm handling this better than I thought I would. If there is no concert, then we will adjust. It was planned to be a good thing for Dianne, but if surgery is the better thing, then let it be. I just hate all this. Vonda asked me at work if I was dealing with Dianne's condition and I said 'probably not', I guess its time for me to start."

"Honey, I think you are dealing with it all. How you can handle what you do is beyond me. I just hope I haven't done something wrong by letting Charles send this message through me."

"No, Alex, you did just fine." A few minutes later he was gone.

The pain he left behind was close to unbearable. Laura talked to David and Dylan. The knowing and the not knowing were hard to deal with. Plans were not possible so Laura shed a few tears, did some serious praying and put her head on the pillow.

Friday passed slowly. No word from Dianne. When the workday ended Laura gathered everything she could possibly think for the weekend, just in case. Then she got the last minute phone call.

Dianne had been the holdup. She was really upset and told her doctor that her quality of life should count for something. She said, "What possible difference could one week make? Laura and I have been going to this concert for years and this year I have a chance to go with my whole family." Dianne won. The surgery was set for the week after the concert. It would be at Duke.

The concert date soon arrived. There were four rooms reserved in Raleigh and everyone met up the afternoon of the concert. In order not to miss a trick, everyone ate at the concert. There were two seats with the two wheel chair places. Charles was not about to leave Dianne so Laura alternated her seat with Dylan and Kevin. When she was not with David she was with Alex and whoever was using the other two seats. It was a great time as all Buffett concerts are. Afterwards while the old folks rested the young ones went out in search of food. The next morning everyone met for breakfast and then headed for home. It was a milestone in celebrating life.

Monday following the concert was surgery day. Laura had a motel room close to the hospital in case she needed to stay and to give David a place to rest during the surgery. By this time he could get himself to the commode if someone got him to the bathroom. Laura knew that Dylan could handle this while she was in the waiting room. When they called for the family, Laura talked to the doctor, as she did not have a clue where Charles was. Later, he was found sound asleep with his head resting against a post. She knew, first hand, how tired he must be. This time they got more of the tumor and planted Chemo wafers and even attacked the root that was near the spinal chord. Dianne came through like her tough self. She was walking in three days and gone home in four. She did not suffer from double vision like she did after the first surgery.

David was beginning to walk on his own. He got his driver's license back and was thrilled. His fixator kept him from going many places or driving as much as he wanted, but it was wonderful having him drive again. His goal was to be out of his wheelchair before he started back to school. He had made up his social studies and Algebra III. It looked as if he would definitely graduate with his class. He still had no use of his left hand. Laura prayed everyday for him to be healed.

About a week before his senior year they decided to remove David's fixator. He had been having procedures done on it all along. It was originally two metal rods on the outside of his leg but attached to his bones by screws through his skin. One procedure changed it from two rods to one. Other procedures relocated the pin sites for better healing. Altogether, there had been about 12 procedures on his leg. This would hopefully be the last and his leg, the one he was supposed to lose, would be pronounced well. Dr. Wittenberg was always glad to see David. This time he said, "Man, it's good to see you. I always like to see what a walking miracle looks like." The procedure was pretty painful and Laura was very glad that they had taken such good care of those pin sites all this time. They did not give David anything for pain, but Laura had taught David the breathing exercises she had learned in Lamaze classes for just such an occasion. So while David was saying his "Ah, Hees" Dr. Wittenberg was unscrewing his pins from his leg bones with a hand drill. Mercy. That afternoon David had an appointment to get his senior pictures taken.

On August 9, 1999 David entered Caldwell High as a senior. The morning went very well. David dressed himself and even ate a little breakfast. His book bag was packed the night before. There were only two small snags. One, David forgot his glasses, and two; his car was a bit short on gas. Laura and Dylan followed him to the gas station and Dylan put the gas in for him. What a family! David was all set. He had a cane with a very large rectangular base and his book bag was all set to go. He could not carry the book bag and use the cane but they were not worried. When they got to school Nancy carried his bag and David walked into the school. David walked into the school. David walked into the school. Praise the Lord! Laura took pictures of them all the way in. She sat in the car for a few minutes. She paused a moment to thank the Lord for these two fine young men. Her sister was still not in pain, her boys were in school, Alex loved her, and her bills were paid, God was surely in His heaven.

Laura took Dylan to school for his first day in the eighth grade. She was very proud of this young man and tried her best to show it among all the tumult. It was also the first day for the new middle school. People had been fighting to have this school built since 1976. She was glad that Dylan would have a chance to go there. Sometimes she questioned her decision about leaving this school for a job at Central Office eight years before. She really could not doubt the move now, however, because her new job had allowed her the flexibility to help with David.

On the evening of August 17th Charles called to say that the chemo was working and there had been zero growth of the tumor since the surgery. Dianne was feeling much better so they began to plan a party. Walker was planning to marry Holly at the end of September. As far as Laura could discern no one was doing anything for the couple. This was Holly's second marriage and she wanted a very small wedding. Her parents were elderly and not even planning to come to the wedding. Walker's mother wasn't doing anything. Laura had heard that Walker and Holly were going to the beach for a weekend in a couple of weeks. Laura made Walker promise to come by and see Dianne before they headed back. Walker said that he was definitely planning on that. In fact, they wanted to come by on Saturday. So they set the time for Saturday at three.

Dianne and Laura set about planning the cake cutting. Laura took everything that was not already at Dianne's. She ordered a wedding cake from a bakery in Wilmington. She gathered the candles, tablecloth, flowers, and trimmings. She baked the food and made the salads. The table looked great. Grandmaw's punch bowl was on one end and the cake on the other. The food was delicious. Everyone was together for the celebration of life. Walker and Holly were astounded.

September was a very busy month. Laura and Dylan actually got to go to the river cabin for a few hours over Labor Day. It was one of Dylan's favorite places in the world but they had only been there a couple of times all summer. They only made one trip to Wilmington during September. More would have been scheduled but too much happened. Aunt Cathy passed away. She had always been such a support to Laura and her family.

Her memorial service was scheduled on the same day as Walker's wedding. To top it all off, David was in the homecoming court and had to be back at school at one o'clock. Dianne and Charles spent the night at Laura's. They left the next morning for the graveside service. David and Dylan were following. The whole family met at the church for lunch and a memorial service was to follow. David and Dylan returned to Caldwell High for the ceremony and Laura, Dianne, and Charles headed for Walker's wedding. Celebrate! And celebrate somemore!

Then things seemed to calm down a bit. David was not in therapy at the moment, although the exercises continued at home. He began driving himself to school. Nancy met him each day to carry his books. He could take care of most of his needs and was getting more and more independent. Dylan was getting along fine. Dianne was holding steady and Laura was taking it all in. The house was still filled with teenagers every night and the trips to Wilmington continued.

The school sent Laura a notice that it was time to send in what they wanted on the back pages of the annual. After several days of serious thought, Laura sent in the following two page ads. The first page was surrounded with pictures of David from the time he was little until his graduation picture. The second page had pictures of David's car, hospital and progress until he was walking with a cane.

The first page with the growing-up pictures read:

Dearest David,
You have walked with the Lord.
You have passed the test of caring and sharing.
You have passed the test of taking care of others.
You have passed the test of determination.
You have passed the test of endurance.
You have passed the test of self-control.

You have passed the test of humiliation.
You have passed the test of pain.
You have passed the test of survival.
You have passed the test of peer pressure.
You have passed the test of responsibility.
You have passed the test of hard work.
You have passed the test of smiling.
You have passed more tests than most people do in a lifetime.
You have walked with the Lord.

Now, as you graduate from Caldwell High and continue down life's path, we wish you health, happiness, and even more love. You deserve it.

Who loves you? We do!!!!!! Mom, Dad, and Dylan

And the second page with the wreck and healing pictures read:

The family of David McDowell

Thanks you for your
Every act of kindness and
Your every prayer.
We wish you a safe
And happy future.
Please drive carefully.

It was about this time that Alex became dissatisfied. He was upset because Laura would not take a weekend trip with him and because she wasn't paying enough attention to his family. Laura tried to explain that there was no way she could leave David for the weekend. She also explained that with the year that they had been through she really didn't think that it had been enough time for her to start being more active in his family. He insisted, so Laura sent a fall plant to his mom and started buying Christmas presents for the whole gang.

They went to Wilmington for Thanksgiving. Charles was glad for a little break to go hunting. David could help with the driving. Laura could sit and visit with her wonderful sister.

Christmas was magical again. Laura had a big Christmas dinner for Walker and Holly, Susan and her boyfriend, David and Dylan. They left on the twenty-sixth for a few days in Wilmington.

January was a disaster for Alex and Laura. First he was mad because he would try to call and could not get through. Someone was always on the Internet and, at that time, dialup was all they had. Then he really got upset one night when Laura was going to be late getting to his house. Dylan was expecting a friend from out of town to spend the night. His parents were pulling a massive trailer on the way to town and it was taking longer than expected because the mountain roads were bad. She had to pick this child up when they got to town due to the trailer and all. Finally, when they had not arrived and it was seven-thirty, Laura called Alex to say that there was no way she would be there for dinner. He told her not to come at all. She said that she was sorry and thought that everything was under control. The next day about five, when she had not heard from Alex, she called him again. "I just want to check to be sure that we still had plans for tonight."

He replied, "After the way you treated me last night, I don't think so."

"Okay, I'm sorry about last night. I really thought you understood the situation." Let's all keep in mind here that Laura was driving to Alex's every Friday and Saturday night. He had made no effort to change that or do the driving to her house.

"What I understand is that you do not have time in your life for a man."

"Well, okay, if that's how you feel."

"That's how I feel."

"Okay." Laura got off the phone and told her boys that she would not be seeing Alex. They were not the least bit upset. She got her book and stretched out in her bed to read. She was surprised at how nice it was to relax. She figured that Alex was right.

The whole family gathered at Laura's cousin's house to celebrate David's eighteenth birthday on February 5th.

David was questioning his reason for living. Did the Lord really save him for a purpose? If so, what was it? When would he know what he was supposed to do? Why did Steven seem to have it made? Laura answered as best she could. She reassured David that the Lord did have a plan for him. She said that for right now they needed to continue to focus on getting David well and seeing to his education. "Revenge is mine" sayeth the Lord. We don't need to be concerned with Steven. The Lord will take care of Steven.

At Rehab they had met a young man who had been in a motorcycle accident and had lost both his legs. He and David shared a long conversation one day about the differences between friends and acquaintances. The man told David that he had not lost any friends but he had lost some acquaintances. David really took this to heart. Later that day he and Laura had a very serious discussion.

"I don't think that I've lost any friends."

"No, I don't think so either," was Laura's reply.

"I know that there are people I can always count on. I know that I can always count on you."

Laura thought about this for a minute and said to David, "Well, I would like to think that you could always count on me. I will certainly make every effort to be there for you. But you never know what might happen. I know that there are two things you can always count on."

"What would that be?"

"One, you can always count on change, and two, you can always count on the Lord."

On Wednesday, February 9th, Laura gave Dianne a call to see how an MRI had gone and what report they had received from Duke. Brad answered the phone. The report was not good. Brad explained, "The tumor is growing and there is a second tumor or another part of the first tumor growing from the roots at the back of her brain. It was about 20% the size of the original tumor. They took her off the old chemo and are starting her on a chemo pill. I think it has about a 25% success rate and is real strong. Let's see. She will take it here. She doesn't have to go to the hospital. The problem is the pill is so strong that she might not tolerate it to begin with".

Laura could sense the despair in Brad's voice and ended the conversation quickly. She told Brad that she would see them over the weekend.

There was a big difference in Dianne. Occasionally, her legs would go weak. Charles asked Laura to bring her mother's wheelchair. Dianne would sit in front of the TV, but she could not concentrate. She was very quiet. Dianne had never been quiet in her life. Laura sat with her and they made Valentine key chains for Kevin and Brad. Laura knew that the time had to be drawing close, but she could not stand to think about it. They had spent almost a year celebrating everything and this was very, very sad.

On April 6, the results of the MRI scan showed shrinkage in the original tumor and no growth in the new tumor. Praise the Lord.

Dianne spent much of the week before Easter in the hospital. She was so weak from the chemo that, even though it was shrinking the original tumor and keeping the second one at bay, it seemed to be doing as much harm as good. Charles was distraught. A doctor had talked to him about stopping the chemo and giving Dianne some quality of life. When he talked to Laura, he said he wanted her to think about it so they could discuss it when she got there. One thing for sure, no one would give Dianne chemo in her present condition.

When they arrived in Wilmington for Easter, Dianne was worse. She would barely talk. She refused to take medicine. She could not walk.

They were finding cancer in other parts of her body. Easter was still a celebration, but much subdued. A dark cloud was hanging overhead. The only bright spot was that David was getting better. He still could not use his hand and was headed for some more therapy, but he was beginning to take some steps without any support. His goal was to walk all the way across the stage at graduation without a cane.

Alex was history. He told Laura one evening after fixing her a good steak dinner that he needed to go on a vacation. He had not been on a vacation in so long and just could not go by himself so he wanted her to go with him. He had to have someone go with him and he wanted it to be her. Laura repeated about how she felt about traveling with him with so many things going on in her life. Finally, she said, "Alex, would you come to my house, sleep in my bed, and get up the next morning and eat breakfast with my boys?"

"Hell, no."

"Well, what you are asking me to do is something that you are not willing to do."

Laura gathered her things and left. It was the last time she spoke to Alex.

David was to graduate on May 23rd. Laura sent out invitations to friends, relatives, and fellow workers. She also included invitations to lunch at a close by restaurant. Gifts and acceptances came pouring in. The local newspaper printed the following article:

> David McDowell will graduate May 23 like other seniors. What sets him apart from classmates is two years ago doctors didn't expect him to survive a head-on collision.
>
> "He is a remarkable young man," said Mr. Thomas, Caldwell High School principal, "He's determined and positive."
>
> "We were told he wasn't going to live," said Laura McDowell, David's mother. "But we had thousands of people praying for him."

David will walk across a stage at Caldwell High School football stadium to receive his diploma. He hopes to do it without using his walking cane.

"His goal is to walk without his cane for graduation." Laura said. "After that his goal is to get back 110 percent."

On September 23, 1998, David was in a 70-mile-per-hour head-on collision with another student driving a borrowed car. He was leaving school to go to work.

David was airlifted to Carolinas Medical Center. His right leg was shattered and his left arm fractured, his mother said. The only thing he could move was his right hand. He also had a blood clot in his brain. She was told that, if he lived, he would lose his leg.

"He had surgery on his leg," Laura said. "He had to relearn a lot of things as a result of the blood clot in his brain."

He went straight from the hospital to Charlotte Rehab, she said. He came home in a wheelchair in December. He could stand and, with help, he could take some steps. He still cannot use his left hand, she said.

"He fought every inch of the way," she said. "I believe that he has been an inspiration to a lot of people."

When he returned to school, he attended three classes each morning and continued going to rehabilitation every afternoon. For the time he was out of school, he lost four credits. He made up two of them at home.

"David has clearly shown he's a strong-willed young man to come back from a tragic situation," said Thomas. "He is a shining example of someone setting a goal and accomplishing it."

Now David has been accepted at the University of North Carolina at Charlotte in mechanical engineering. He plans to start classes in the fall.

After being told repeatedly her son would not live, how does Laura feel about David's life being spared?

"I cannot think of words that could possibly express how I feel," she said. "But I thank the Lord every day."

Graduation time was fast approaching. Laura was wondering if she had bitten off more than she could chew. On Tuesday Laura called Dianne. She said that Charles was washing her hair and she would call back in the afternoon. Charles called to say that he thought Dianne was slipping into a coma. She was becoming more lethargic every day. Laura offered to come down. Charles said, "No, Laura, you have done everything you could possibly do. You need to be with David now and see him through graduation." Dianne went to sleep on that Tuesday afternoon and did not get out of bed again.

Laura was beside herself. She would call. You could talk to Dianne and she would wiggle her foot as if to say that she was hearing you. Laura kept offering to come down because she felt like she should be with her sister and Charles kept saying that it was not what she should do.

At the awards ceremony on Wednesday, David received the Sandy Nininger Award from the Kiwanis club. This award would pay for college tuition and fees. What an answer to prayers.

On Thursday Charles called to say that things were very bad. Hospice had been there with all kinds of instructions and Dianne's best friend, Patsy, was standing by. Laura was so sad. Truly, truly, sad. She asked Patsy to put the phone to her sister's ear and said, "You know I love you and I know that you love me. If I do not see you tomorrow, I know that you will see me." Dianne wiggled her foot and Laura got off the phone.

They had to leave for the stadium by 8:30 the next morning to get seats for graduation. At seven Charles called to say that Dianne had passed away at 5:30. Laura told Charles that she would be there as soon as she could. He told her not to rush. Receiving would be on Saturday night with the Memorial Service on Sunday. Laura passed the bad news on to her boys. They got themselves together, held up their heads, and left for graduation.

Somehow, by the time they found some seats, most everyone knew about Dianne. Most of the family found seats close by, but a few were scattered all around. The athletic director gave David a ride to his seat in the school's golf cart. They had also built a special rail so David could hold on with his right hand going up on the stage and coming down. Pretty soon, all the other graduates marched in. It was a beautiful, warm, sunny, Friday morning. Laura felt like she would make it through the ceremony just fine. She was a little surprised when Channel Eight news showed up.

Laura was totally composed when the Valedictorian got up to speak. Her speech began with, "When we were freshmen we got back our Victory bell and decided not to ever let it go again. When we were sophomores we were all in a hurry to get our license before the new restrictions took place. When we were juniors David McDowell was in a wreck and we all learned what was meant by determination…" Well, that was the end of Laura's composure. Sharon went on to say many more nice things about David and how he had been an inspiration.

Soon it was time for the graduates to receive the diplomas and one by one the names were called. When they called David's name, the crowd was very quiet. David did exactly as he wanted. He walked up to the stage, walked across it, got his diploma, and walked down the steps. As he did this, the students stood up and clapped. The teachers joined in. Then the entire stadium full of people stood up and cheered for the ovation. Laura was so proud, deeply moved, deeply thankful, and felt her sister's presence.

At the end of the ceremony everyone was crowding out onto the field. For just an instance, Laura and Dylan were left alone. Laura felt a strange sensation and put her hand on Dylan's shoulder for support. These words came out of her mouth, "Well, Mister Dylan, how do you feel about having a brother graduated from high school?" Dylan looked a little perplexed because it was not something his Mom would say, and then she continued, "Well, I want you to work real hard so you will graduate someday too." And with that the strange feeling and strange words were gone. Laura looked at Dylan and said, "I don't think that was me. I think that was Dianne talking to you." Dylan nodded his head.

There was great commotion on the field with lots of pictures. There was a great gathering of family and friends for lunch. Even at home there were people coming by. Some were coming to celebrate; some were coming to offer condolences. Vonda came by from work with food to cover the next day or two. It was well into the late evening before things settled down. Laura got to watch David graduate again on the news. They had interviewed him after the ceremony and David shared his plans about going to the beach. Laura decided to let David have his day and they could leave for Wilmington in the morning.

Charles and his boys seemed very glad to see them when they arrived. Several of Charles's family members were already there. Most of Dianne's would be coming on Sunday. Laura was glad she had brought all the food. They needed it.

Dianne's wishes were to be cremated and her ashes scattered over the ocean. Charles had her dressed for the occasion. She had on her bucket hat that she had worn since the time she had lost her hair and, much to Laura's delight, a Jimmy Buffett tee shirt.

Laura did not know many people at the receiving until she turned around to find three of her friends from Caldwell Middle School. She was in total surprise that someone would travel that far. It really made her feel good.

Charles was never one to keep things so she stayed an extra day to help him go through all of Dianne's belongings. He sent as much as Laura could pack in her car home for Laura to use. He left too. He spent about six months in Colorado trying to get himself together.

When Laura, David, and Dylan returned home, there was still much to do. There were thank you notes, orientations, and Laura still had to work. David had to take the math test a couple of times so they could place him in the right class. He would have to go to summer school and it started July 5th. Registrations had to be completed and books purchased.

The family decided that they would spend the 3rd, 4th, and 5th at the river cabin. A couple of extra friends came with them. It was the most perfect Fourth of July Laura could ever remember. After playing in the water all day, they headed up to the bridge for the fireworks show. They got there in time to eat supper at the Japanese steak house. Their parking was good enough that they could sit in the car for the show. The fireworks were synchronized with music from a local radio station. It was the best show they had ever seen.

David and the friends left for home after the show. David was going to get himself up for his first college class all by himself and leave his Mom at the river cabin for a day of rest. Laura was uneasy, but David assured her that it was what he needed to do.

Laura was very relieved to talk to David after class. All had gone well. He had found the disability parking and had gotten to class just fine. It was a much better scenario than orientation had been, when David had fallen down trying to get to a class.

Laura relaxed for the rest of the day. She played in the water with Dylan. They took turns on the jet ski and ate junky food. One of Laura's passions was to watch the sun go down at the river. It set right across the channel. Dylan suggested that she take the Jet Ski out and watch the sunset from the middle of the lake.

Out in the middle of the channel watching that beautiful scene, with the pinks and purples from the sky reflecting across the water and the sun's last glow creating all the sparkles across the water, Laura was able to pull many thoughts together. She was thankful for the incomparable beauty around her, the peace and quiet of the moment, the loving child that was waiting for her on the dock, the miracle child that had made it through his first day of college, the wonderful parents and sister she had, the family and friends who had stuck by her, her job, her home, her river cabin, her health, her Lord God Almighty and His Precious Son who had seen her through the hard times. Still, she knew that there would be more rough times ahead, but she relaxed and thought of all the things she practiced to keep herself in line. She knew that they should be included in the book, so she has listed them for you. She also remembered what she had said to David about what you can always count on, "You can count on two things. You can count on change and you can count on the Lord."

## THE END

Here is a list of things to do when your outlook is dim. They are not listed in order of importance or what works best. They are listed as they occurred to me.

Always count your blessings and praise the Lord.

Get out of bed. Bed is great until your thoughts take you to depression. It can happen in a flash, and then you are stuck and do not want to get up. So, put your feet on the floor, get yourself dressed, have a cup of coffee or your morning wake-me-up of choice.

If you are really down, find someone to talk to. If you can, pick the person carefully. Find someone who is positive by nature. They can probably shed light on a situation that has not occurred to you. If there is no one at your disposal, go shopping. If you only have $2, spend time looking for something for $1.25 then buy a store-brand drink from a machine. When you leave the store, someone will probably say, "Have a good day". When they do, it will feel like manna from heaven. It is amazing what those words can do for you when you are down and out.

Once you notice this, never fail to say the same to others. If they say, "Good morning", reply "And the rest of the day to you."

Pray to the Lord. Always begin with something you are thankful for. Pretty soon, your communication with the Lord will set your mind at ease. Pray for peace, wisdom, and strength. You will receive it. Pray for the people who need help.

Read the Bible. Read John 14 and John 15. Read Psalm 23 and 34. If it is hard to get started, keep it simple. Read just a little bit. It will get easier, become a comfort and be enjoyable.

Listen to music. Sing. Dance with the mop. Change partners and dance with the broom.

Take on new projects. You can't take on big projects while someone is sick in the hospital, but you can take on little ones, ones that you can carry with you to work on.

Always have something with you to do while you are waiting. The secret to having patience is having something to do in the meantime. Never just sit.

Give yourself 24 hours. If a problem looms gigantic after 24 hours, then find a way to deal with it rationally.

When the crisis hits or while you are absorbing the crisis, continue to do what you were doing. If you were doing nothing, make a pitcher of tea.

Make a list of things to do. Be sure to put on the list some of the things you have already done and check them off.

Help someone else in any way you can.

Listen to others.

If someone you love has a problem with drugs or alcohol go to Alanon meetings.

At one point, when Laura was so upset over David, she actually screamed at the top of her lungs as she drove to Rehab. She did not know she could scream so loudly or so long. Her throat hurt a little when she finished, but the tightness in her chest was gone. She only recommends screaming on very rare occasions. Someone might have you committed.

Read or watch something funny. Laughter is a great reliever (better than screaming).

Go to the Internet. Watch something funny.

Color a picture with bright colors.

Practice good breathing. Go for a walk.

Write a book.

Made in the USA
Coppell, TX
10 November 2026

11835570R00132